THE
IRON
TRIANGLE

Inside the Secret World of the
Carlyle Group

DAN BRIODY

WILEY

JOHN WILEY & SONS, INC.

Published by John Wiley & Sons, Inc., Hoboken, New Jersey.
Published simultaneously in Canada.

For general information on our other products and services, or technical support,
please contact our Customer Care Department within the United States at
800-762-2974, outside the United States at 317-572-3993 or fax 317-572-4002.

Wiley also publishes its books in a variety of electronic formats. Some content that
appears in print may not be available in electronic books. For more information about
Wiley products, visit our Web site at www.wiley.com.

ISBN 0-471-28108-5

Printed in the United States of America.

10 9 8 7 6 5 4 3 2

CONTENTS

FOREWORD

At the dawn of the third millennium, as the nation prepares for its second war in the Persian Gulf in little more than 10 years, the same debate rages in this country that has defined it for the last three centuries: What exactly does it mean to be an American? Is America a place or a state of mind?

The British may love their language, and the French may love their gold, but Americans love more than anything to argue over who they really are. And in all that time, and all that arguing— from the dueling essays of Jefferson and Hamilton, to the confused politics of the Reform Party and Pat Buchanan—the American story has ultimately never strayed very far from the plotline that has energized it from the start.

You may devote a lifetime to peeling back the onion skins of the American Experience, as so many scholars have done, and no matter where you stop you will always encounter the same basic question that frames our history: In a democracy, what are the limits to legitimate power?

At its core, that is the question that informs *The Iron Triangle: Inside the Secret World of the Carlyle Group*—just as it eventually seems to inform our understanding of everything that ever happens in American public life, from the XYZ Affair to the Pentagon Papers. It is why one generation of Americans enacts the Sherman Antitrust Act, and a later generation eviscerates it. At the start of the 1950s, a screenwriter named Ring Lardner, Jr. was imprisoned as a Communist sympathizer; a generation later he was lionized in Hollywood as the screenwriter of M*A*S*H.

Of such moments is the history of this country eventually told, as Americans engage in the ceaseless pursuit of midcourse corrections to get where we want to go as a nation without becoming a tyranny in the process. When Richard Nixon lamented the nation's seeming obsession with "wallowing in Watergate," he missed the key point: As a nation and a people, we really had no other choice.

Now, in the winter of 2003, with America's wrath once again poised to strike down Iraq, a palpable sense is abroad in the land—not shared by all, but shared by enough—that we have somehow drawn a line in the sand where we never really intended to stand. How did we get to this moment anyway? In the visible mechanism of political cause and effect, part of what's happening feels hidden from view. We see the cause, and we see the effect. But the assembly of gears that transmits the power seems off somewhere else, in another room.

It is the work of scholarship—and in particular, of that uniquely American kind of contemporary scholarship that we call investigative journalism—to enter those darkened rooms and switch on the light so that all may see what is actually taking place. When the work is done well, and the message is true, we find ourselves in a diorama we never imaged could exist. One thinks in that regard of Jacob A. Riis's *How the Other Half Lives,* or more recently, and on a different stage entirely, Wise and Ross's *Invisible Government.* At other times, the exposes connect invisible dots, and in fairly short order are deservedly consigned to the ash bin of history as conspiracy theory. (Want to find yourself standing alone at a cocktail party? Then try suggesting that you have it on good authority that the Trilateral Commission actually runs the world.)

Briody's scholarship will meet no such fate, for not only are the facts of *The Iron Triangle* accurate, but the picture they present is also *true.* And just as *Invisible Government* in 1964 helped bring depth to our understanding of some of the missing gears that soon drove America into the jungles and highlands of Indochina, so too does *The Iron Triangle* introduce us to the men (and they are mostly just that) whose role in the geopolitics of the Middle East is now only glimpsed fleetingly, and never by design.

In the foreign policy apparatus of Washington, the Carlyle Group inhabits one of the most darkened rooms of all—hiding in plain sight in offices a mere five minutes' walk down Pennsylvania Avenue from the White House. Into this room, Briody has wandered uninvited and flipped on the light, to reveal the entire spin-cycle apparatus of post-public-sector employment that keeps the top men of successive administrations still gainfully employed in the fields they know best (typically aerospace and defense) once the boss has vacated the White House and returned to private life.

In this room, you'll meet the crude and brashly entertaining original founder of the Carlyle Group, Stephen Norris, a one-time hotel executive for the Marriott Corporation, who figured out how to exploit a late-1980s tax break passed for some Eskimos whose businesses kept failing, and parlayed it into a gimmick for monetizing the value of failure itself, and then marketing it as tax loss carry-forwards.

From this gimmick sprang the Carlyle Group—named by Norris and some chums after an organizing meeting they'd held in New York's Carlyle Hotel, as if the Group were nothing more than a piece of faux Regency furniture in need of a credential.

In these pages, you'll meet the relentlessly over-achieving David Rubenstein, now no longer the boy wonder bullet-biter of the Carter White House, where he held the title of Deputy Domestic Policy Assistant at the age of 27, and was said to have eaten three squares a day, for the entire four years, on junk food from White House vending machines.

You'll also come face-to-face with hatchet-faced Frank Carlucci ("Spooky Frank"), a man with a shadowy past including allegations that he began his career in the CIA with a foiled attempt to assassinate Patrice Lumumba in the Eisenhower years—something that Spooky Frank denies. You'll see him rise to deputy director of the CIA late in the Carter years, then "retire" early in the first term of Ronald Reagan's administration to become head of Sears World Trade—a company with a business that consisted, intriguingly, of neither deals nor revenues. Then, drawn back to Washington by the Great Revolving Door of government, Carlucci took a seat on the National Security Council, once again for Ronald Reagan, then hopped over to Defense, finally spinning back through the door and into the private sector. At the end of Reagan's second term, he was settling behind his desk at the Carlyle Group.

You'll meet such figures as George Bush, Sr.'s one-time secretary of state, James Baker, who also joined the team, and even the ex-president himself, now a senior advisor to the Group.

And, for the first time anywhere, you'll go behind the scenes to see what this group really does as a "business." How it nails down deals, whose arms get twisted, and why. On the light side, you'll encounter comic relief figures like Prince Alwaleed bin Talal, who has promoted himself around the world as a top member of the Saudi royal family but has proved to be a spectacularly inept investor, pouring vast sums of Saudi money into dot-com stocks at the top of the boom.

More darkly, you'll enter the astounding—and until now almost entirely hidden—world of the Vinnell Corporation, which has been training the Saudi Armed Forces in how to protect their country's oil fields since the mid-1970s. There are now an almost unbelievable 45,000 private mercenaries working for Vinnell and outfits like it in place in the country. Vinnell was a Carlyle Group subsidiary from 1992 to 1997.

What is one to make of all this? Certainly enough to want to know more, which is why a book such as *The Iron Triangle* is such an important contribution: It puts the subject in play. A half century ago, Douglas MacArthur, having been summoned back to Washington from Korea by his Commander in Chief, Harry Truman, and relieved of his command over a dispute regarding his conduct of the war, stood before a joint session of Congress and declared, in one of the most memorable moments in American life, that "old soldiers never die, they just fade away . . ." after which he retired to the penthouse suite of the Waldorf Astoria Hotel in New York and was rarely seen in public again. Today, he would more likely have retired to the Carlyle Group, where he'd find a reporter named Dan Briody dogging his every move.

—CHRISTOPHER BYRON

March 2003

TIME LINE

February 1975—Vinnell Corp., a construction contractor and future Carlyle company, signs a $77 million contract to train the Saudi Arabian National Guard. The news touches off a controversy that would dog Vinnell, and then later Carlyle, to the present day, even after Carlyle sold off Vinnell to TRW in the mid-1990s.

December 1986—Frank Carlucci is named national security advisor to President Ronald Reagan, succeeding John Poindexter, who resigned in disgrace following the Iran-Contra scandal. While waiting to assume his responsibilities as national security advisor, Carlucci is briefly embroiled in an arms scandal of his own, when the *Washington Post* reports that Sears World Trade was involved in clandestine international arms deals while Carlucci was chairman.

September 1987—After making millions brokering deals that exploited an obscure tax loophole, Stephen Norris and David Rubenstein form the Carlyle Group, named after the posh Carlyle Hotel on New York's Upper East Side.

November 1987—Frank Carlucci is named secretary of defense by President Ronald Reagan. During his short tenure, Carlucci worked extensively on restructuring the Pentagon's procurement system, a system he would later exploit as chairman of the Carlyle Group.

July 1988—BDM, soon to be a Carlyle company, is accused by rivals of currying favor with the Navy officer in charge of procurement, Melvyn Paisley, by hiring his wife. Paisley would go on to become the highest profile conviction of Operation Ill Wind, the years-long investigation into corruption at the Pentagon.

September 1988—Fred Malek resigns as chairman of the Republican National Committee after reports that while a Nixon aide, he compiled figures on the number of Jews working in the Bureau of Labor and Statistics. He immediately signs on with Carlyle.

January 1989—Six days after his term as secretary of defense ended, Frank Carlucci joins the Carlyle Group.

July 1989—Marriott Corp. sells its In-Flite Services catering business to Marriott's upper management. Carlyle invests in the deal, renames the company Caterair, and loses millions when the airline catering business evaporates in the early 1990s.

February 1990—George W. Bush joins Caterair board at the behest of Fred Malek, a good friend of his father's. Bush would later drop his disastrous experience with Caterair from his resume when he runs for governor of Texas in 1994.

September 1990—Carlyle Group buys BDM Consulting, one of the largest and most successful defense consultancies in the world. Carlyle would use the $130 million purchase to evaluate future buyouts in the defense industry.

January 1991—After months of contentious negotiations, Carlyle snags a board seat at Harsco, a maker of military vehicles. The seat would eventually help Carlyle to obtain Harsco's defense business, later known as United Defense.

February 1991—Prince Alwaleed of Saudi Arabia buys $590 million of stock in Citicorp, America's largest bank. Carlyle brokers the deal and gains a reputation as the merchant bank of choice for wealthy Saudis.

March 1992—BDM, a Carlyle company, buys Vinnell, a privatized military training company that does extensive work with the Saudi Arabian National Guard.

August 1992—Carlyle wins a year-long struggle over control of LTV Corp.'s defense and aerospace division, paying $475 million in conjunction with Loral Corp. and Northrop Corp. The deal instantly legitimizes Carlyle as a serious player in defense buyouts.

September 1992—George Soros, a future Carlyle investor, brings the British economy to its knees by speculating on the demise of the British pound. When the value of the pound cratered on Black Wednesday, September 16, 1992, Soros pocketed a cool billion.

February 1993—A month after the Bush administration cleans out its desks at the White House, Richard Darman, the outgoing director of the Office of Management and Budget, joins the Carlyle Group in a package deal with James Baker III.

March 1993—After spending 12 straight years in the White House in various capacities under Reagan and Bush, James Baker III takes his considerable talents to the Carlyle Group, lending the firm instant international recognition and credibility.

September 1993—Carlyle snags its highest profile investor to date when George Soros invests $100 million in Carlyle Partners II, a fund that would go on to become the biggest and most successful of all Carlyle's funds.

December 1994—A *Washington Post* article exposes a secret arms deal conducted by BDM, a Carlyle company. In the deal, BDM used the same arms broker from the Iran-Contra scandal to arrange the transfer of Russian military equipment to the United States.

January 1995—Co-founder Stephen Norris is forced out of the company, accused by his colleagues of erratic behavior and fiscal irresponsibility. Norris faults his former colleagues for waging a smear campaign against him, spreading rumors and undermining his credibility to the financial community.

March 1995—University of Texas Investment Management Company, UTIMCO, weeks after George W. Bush became governor of Texas, places a $10 million investment into the Carlyle Group, which up until 1994, employed the young Bush.

September 1995—Onex Food Services buys Caterair from Carlyle for $500 million, nearly $150 million less than Carlyle had originally paid for the company.

November 1995—A car bomb attack on Americans living in Saudi Arabia puts a spotlight on Vinnell, BDM, and the presence of the Carlyle Group in Saudi Arabia. Three spouses of BDM workers are injured in the attack.

September 1996—Carlyle closes Carlyle Partners II at a total of $1.33 billion, more than twice its original target for the fund, and 13 times as much as the company had ever raised for a single fund. The defense-oriented fund would go on to produce returns of better than 35 percent.

September 1997—Carlyle buys United Defense for $850 million, one of the company's largest buyouts ever. United Defense has plans to build the Army a 60-ton mobile howitzer called Crusader.

March 1998—John Major, former prime minister of the United Kingdom, joins Carlyle as European advisor. He would later become chairman of Carlyle Europe in May 2001.

April 1998—Carlyle closes another $1.1 billion fund, called Carlyle European Capital Partners, at double its initial target. The company was able to raise the money in just under a year.

May 1999—Former President George Herbert Walker Bush visits South Korea on behalf of Carlyle, cultivating business and political ties that result in Carlyle's investing more than $1 billion in South Korea's struggling economy.

July 1999—Former Connecticut State Treasurer Paul Silvester is forced to resign his new position at Park Strategies after the FBI begins an investigation into a series of investments he made with Connecticut State Pension funds before he left office. Among the investments is a $50 million placement with Carlyle Asia.

September 1999—Silvester pleads guilty to corruption. Court documents are sealed, and the identities of the private equity firms involved are kept secret by the state, awaiting Silvester's sentencing, which is ongoing.

January 2001—SBC Communications, a Carlyle client, wins FCC approval to offer long-distance phone service in Texas, Oklahoma, and Kansas, after the Justice Department had rejected the company's request. The approval is given on the last day of FCC Chairman William Kennard's tenure. Three months later, Kennard is given a job at Carlyle.

February 2001—George W. Bush, a month into his presidency, reverses America's policy of diplomacy toward North Korea, angering North and South Koreans alike, and threatening Carlyle's extensive investments in the region.

June 2001—Former President George H. W. Bush urges his son to reconsider his stance on North Korea, reminding him, among other things, of the U.S. business interests in the Korean peninsula. George W. Bush subsequently reverses his policy toward North Korea.

July 2001—Former President George H. W. Bush personally calls Crown Prince Abdullah of Saudi Arabia, reassuring the heir to Saudi Arabia that his son is "going to do the right thing" and "his heart is in the right place." The call is in response to George W. Bush upsetting the Saudi prince with his policy toward the Israeli-Palestinian conflict. It also helps protect Carlyle's extensive business in the region.

September 11, 2001—America sustains a highly organized attack by terrorists, leveling the World Trade Center towers, and ripping a gash in the Pentagon building. The attacks would lead to a massive increase in defense spending. A week after the attacks, Anthrax-laced letters are found throughout the East Coast, leading to heightened fears, and unexpected new contracts for Carlyle companies.

October 2001—Carlyle is forced to liquidate its holdings from the bin Laden family as news reports of the company's association with terrorist Osama bin Laden's estranged family overwhelm the press.

December 2001—Carlyle takes United Defense public after newly approved defense spending temporarily secures the Crusader's future. The company earns $237 million in one day on the sale of shares, and on paper made more than $800 million.

April 2002—Cynthia McKinney, a Democratic congresswoman from Georgia calls for an investigation into the September 11 attacks, pointing out the President's extensive ties with the Carlyle Group, a company that stands to make millions from the aftermath of September 11.

May 2002—The Army is forced to investigate whether its own officials illegally lobbied Congress in support of the Crusader in the face of the program's cancellation.

August 2002—United Defense issues an official press release announcing the cancellation of the Crusader program. The same press release announces the awarding of a new contract for United Defense to build another gun for the Army, effectively replacing Crusader.

November 2002—Lou Gerstner, the man who engineered IBM's stunning turnaround during the 1990s, is hired as Carlyle's chairman. The move is characterized by many in the media to change Carlyle's image from a defense oriented buyout firm to a more traditional private equity company. Frank Carlucci stays on as Chairman Emeritus.

CAST OF CHARACTERS
(in Order of Appearance)

Stephen Norris—co-founder Carlyle Group.

Norris was the driving force behind the creation of the company. A mercurial executive, bent on hunting down big deals, Norris ultimately would be forced out of the firm by his fellow co-founders in an acrimonious conflict.

David Rubentstein—co-founder Carlyle Group.

Still the brains of the operation, Rubenstein is widely considered one of the most intelligent men in Washington, DC. His IQ is surpassed only by his tireless work ethic and extensive Rolodex. He is what holds Carlyle together.

Dan D'Aniello—co-founder Carlyle Group.

A former colleague of Norris at Marriott, D'Aniello was brought on board only after Norris personally guaranteed his salary. He is among the more enigmatic, behind-the-scenes members of Carlyle, often serving as a buffer between the more explosive executives.

William Conway—co-founder Carlyle Group.

The son of a quality control guru and former chief financial officer at MCI, Conway is reputed to be one of the finest financiers in the world. His conservative style and waste-not approach would eventually clash with Norris's larger-than-life personality, resulting in Norris being sent packing.

Frederic Malek—former Carlyle consultant.

This former Nixon aide and close friend of George Bush Sr. ran to Carlyle after a furor erupted in Washington over his involvement in the documented anti-Semitic actions of former President Nixon. He would go on to introduce Carlyle to some big names in Washington, but would later be excommunicated from the firm.

William Barr—former Attorney General.

A one-time law partner of David Rubenstein's, Barr would help Carlyle, along with Rubenstein, funnel millions of dollars through a temporary tax loophole known as the *Great Eskimo Tax Scam,* taking Carlyle into the Big Leagues.

Arthur Miltenberger—then chief investment officer of the Mellon Foundation.

As an original investor in Carlyle Group, Miltenberger was among the first to see the potential of an investment bank based in Washington, DC. His early contributions would get Carlyle on its feet.

J. W. Marriott—chairman of Marriott Corp.

The hotel magnate was once the boss of Steve Norris, Fred Malek, and Dan D'Aniello. The influence of Marriott on Carlyle was a pervasive force, and his former employees still utter his name with the highest respect.

Dan Altobello—former chairman of Caterair.

Yet another former Marriott employee, Altobello had the dubious honor of presiding over one of Carlyle's worst investments ever in Caterair. Like many others, he would clash badly with Norris, and later sell off Caterair at a loss.

George W. Bush—president of the United States of America.

An early hire of Carlyle, Bush was placed on the board of Caterair in 1990 and served for four years, before leaving to run for governor of Texas. His early stint with Carlyle would become a source of controversy later during his presidency.

Frank Carlucci—chairman 1989–2002, currently chairman emeritus of Carlyle Group.

A lifelong public servant, former secretary of defense, former deputy director of the CIA, and more, Frank Carlucci would lead Carlyle into the murky world of defense buyouts in the late 1980s and early 1990s. It is Carlucci's close friendship with Secretary of

Defense Donald Rumsfeld that the press most often seizes on when criticizing Carlyle.

Patrice Lumumba—former president of Zaire.

Assassinated after only two months in power, Lumumba would later become the subject of the film *Lumumba,* directed by Raoul Peck. In the film, there was originally a scene showing Frank Carlucci plotting the murder of the erstwhile leader. The scene was edited at Carlucci's request before the film's release.

Mobuto Sese Seko—former president of Zaire.

Chosen by Americans to succeed Lumumba, Sese Seko led Zaire into decades of famine and war. He remains part of Carlucci's legacy from his time as second secretary to the U.S. Embassy in Zaire.

Raoul Peck—filmmaker.

It was Peck's accounting of the murder of Patrice Lumumba that caused an uproar from Frank Carlucci. At Carlucci's request, Peck edited the scene that showed Carlucci plotting the assassination, but Peck stands by the film's veracity.

Donald Rumsfeld—secretary of defense.

A former college roommate and wrestling teammate of Frank Carlucci, Rumsfeld and Carlucci are never far apart. The two followed each other through the executive ranks of government, worked for Sears Roebuck together, and remain very close friends to this day.

Caspar Weinberger—former secretary of defense.

As one of Carlucci's many mentors, Cap Weinberger helped legitimize Carlucci, grooming him to one day become secretary of defense.

Roderick Hills—former CEO of Sears World Trade.

As the CEO of Sears World Trade, Hills fought off allegations of the company being a front for CIA activity and eventually resigned amidst huge financial losses, leaving Carlucci to succeed him.

Earle Williams—former CEO of BDM.

In leading BDM, a highly successful defense consultancy, Earle Williams curried favor with countless Washington, DC insiders, among them Frank Carlucci. Carlyle would go on to buy BDM and make a killing.

Melvyn Paisley—former Naval officer.

When in the Navy, Paisley was in charge of awarding Navy contracts, a task he did while accepting kickbacks from defense contractors. He would go on to work for BDM, then get convicted after pleading guilty in the Ill Wind investigation into corruption in the Pentagon.

Vicki Paisley—Melvyn's wife.

Also an employee at BDM, Vicki was thought to be the reason that Earle Williams received a highly coveted appointment to the Naval Advisory Board.

Phil Odeen—chairman of TRW.

Williams' successor as BDM CEO, Odeen would grow the company into a highly successful and diversified consultancy. He was also CEO when BDM employees were targeted in a vicious car bombing in Saudi Arabia.

M. W. Gambill—former CEO of defense contractor Harsco.

The CEO of one of Carlyle's early takeover targets, Gambill would fight the fledgling buyout firm for control of Harsco, eventually conceding only a seat on the company's board.

Norman Augustine—former CEO of defense contractor Martin Marietta.

Augustine would go toe-to-toe with Carlyle over the heavily disputed takeover of LTV, an aerospace company spun out of Ford. After a protracted battle, Augustine and Martin Marietta would eventually lose out to Carlyle.

Prince Alwaleed bin Talal—Saudi Arabian prince.

A billionaire international investor, the Prince played a central role in raising Carlyle's name recognition, both at home and in Saudi Arabia. The Prince would go on to become close friends with Steve Norris, and make enormous investments in American companies.

King Fahd—king of Saudi Arabia.

As the leader of Saudi Arabia, King Fahd hired Carlyle companies to protect him and his family, as well as to manage the Saudi Economic Offset Program, a government-run program that brings foreign investment into Saudi Arabia.

Faissel Fahad—San Francisco lawyer.

This friend of Prince Alwaleed was responsible for making the key connection between Carlyle and the Prince, which led to the $590 million investment in Citicorp.

Prince Sultan bin Abdulaziz—Saudi Arabian defense minister.

According to a financial advisor to Prince Alwaleed, Prince Sultan bin Abdulaziz used Prince Alwaleed bin Talal as a front to invest money on his behalf, among others, in U.S. companies, like Citicorp. Prince Alwaleed denies the allegation.

Henry Jackson—former U.S. senator.

Jackson saw early on the perils of letting private companies contract with foreign governments on military missions. His investigation into Vinnell's deal with Saudi Arabia revealed a contract fraught with controversy.

Richard Secord—retired Air Force general.

An ex-employee of Vinnell, but better known as one of the Iran-Contra fall guys, Secord drew unwanted attention to Vinnell when he was implicated in trading arms for hostages.

James Baker III—Carlyle managing director, senior counselor.

The former secretary of state under President George Bush Sr. led five different Republican presidential campaigns, and spent 12 straight years in the White House during the Reagan and Bush administrations. He took a position with Carlyle in 1993, and would later lead George W. Bush's successful battle for the presidency during the Florida recounts.

Richard Darman—Carlyle executive.

The former director of the Office of Management and Budget under Bush Sr., Darman wrangled his way into a position at Carlyle by including himself in a package deal with Baker.

Colin Powell—secretary of state.

A former Carlyle advisor, Powell's role in Carlyle's history is a bit of a mystery. Most believe that he merely advised the company while he was not in public office. One of his early mentors was Frank Carlucci, and the two remain close.

Michael Eisner—chairman of Walt Disney.

Eisner was involved with a deal between Prince Alwaleed and Euro Disney, in which Norris negotiated a huge investment from the Prince. Eisner was among the many that found Norris undisciplined.

Antonio Guizzetti—Italian business man.

After meeting Steve Norris in a sauna at a Washington area gym, Guizzetti led Norris and Baker on a wild tour of Italy in search of the perfect investment. Ultimately, the investment they had targeted fell apart when Norris resigned in the middle of negotiations.

Basil Al Rahim—former Carlyle employee.

In charge of raising capital in Middle East during the early 1990s, Al Rahim was the man who introduced Carlyle to members of the bin Laden family, a relationship that would later cause both parties discomfort.

George Soros—Carlyle investor.

This internationally respected investor and speculator helped legitimize Carlyle when he committed $100 million to the Carlyle Partners II fund. The sizeable investment was accompanied by Soros' public endorsement of Carlyle.

John Major—chairman Carlyle Europe.

The former prime minister of the United Kingdom, Major came on board with Carlyle during a fevered spate of highly political hirings by the company. Since then he has spent time stumping for Carlyle throughout the world.

Paul Silvester—former Connecticut state treasurer.

Silvester is awaiting sentencing after pleading guilty to corruption charges while working as the state treasurer of Connecticut. In his final two months in office, after losing reelection, Silvester invested $800 million of the state's pension fund in several private equity firms for which he received kickbacks. One of the firms he invested in was Carlyle, which was investigated, but no charges were brought.

Wayne Berman—president of Park Strategies.

A consummate Washington insider, Berman is a major financial backer of George W. Bush, as well as the president of Park Strategies, the company that hired Silvester after he invested Connecticut's pension funds through his firm.

Denise Nappier—Connecticut state treasurer.

Stepping into the mess that Silvester left behind, Nappier required that all firms doing business with the Connecticut state pension fund disclose their finder's fee arrangements. After initially holding out, Carlyle disclosed a $1 million fee to Wayne Berman.

Thomas Hicks—founder of Hicks, Muse, Tate & Furst.

This Texas billionaire and George W. Bush backer was responsible for taking the University of Texas' asset management private and investing the school's money with various Republican-friendly firms, including Carlyle.

William Kennard—Carlyle managing director.

The former chairman of the Federal Communications Commission (FCC), Kennard approved a highly questionable bid by SBC Communications, a Carlyle client, to enter into long-distance markets days before he left office. Two months later, he landed a job with Carlyle.

Frank Yeary—Carlyle managing director.

A former investment banker at Salomon Smith Barney, Yeary used his extensive connections at SBC to get Carlyle business there.

Arthur Levitt—Carlyle senior advisor.

The former chairman of the Securities and Exchange Commission (SEC) was known for his policy that protected the individual investor and railed against corporate malfeasance. The irony of his current position with Carlyle is less than subtle.

George Herbert Walker Bush—Carlyle advisor.

The former president of the United States of America has been the source of the majority of Carlyle's controversy. His visits with world business leaders everywhere from Saudi Arabia to South Korea and his repeated influence on American foreign policy make him an easy target for public advocacy groups, who accuse him of influence peddling and damaging conflicts of interest.

Park Tae-joon—Carlyle advisor.

This former prime minister of South Korea was instrumental in securing Carlyle's extensive business interests in the Korean Peninsula.

Michael Kim—Carlyle managing director.

The son-in-law of Park Tae-joon, Kim runs Carlyle's Korean operations, and spearheaded the successful buyout of one of Korea's few healthy banks, KorAm.

Crown Prince Abdullah—heir to the Saudi Arabian throne.

Upset with George W. Bush's pro-Israel policy, Prince Abdullah received a phone call from the president's father, George H. W. Bush, reassuring him that his son was okay, and that George W.'s "heart is in the right place."

Tom Fitton—president of Judicial Watch.

A died-in-the-wool Clinton hater, Fitton caused a stir in Washington when he came out publicly against George H. W. Bush's involvement with the Carlyle Group. His efforts to obtain documents from the federal government have produced some of the most tangible evidence of Carlyle's influence yet.

General Shinseki—U.S. Army chief of staff.

In favor of a more mobile and agile army, General Shinseki originally presented the argument that would ultimately kill United Defense's Crusader, a 42-ton howitzer on wheels.

Andrew Krepinevich—executive director of the Center for Strategic and Budgetary Assessments.

As a member of the Congressionally appointed 1997 National Defense Panel which analyzed military spending, Krepinevich came out against the further development of Crusader, citing the gun's weight and obsolescence as his reasons.

Milo Djukanovic—president of Montenegro.

In searching for support to pursue independence for his country, Djukanovic lobbied the American government to no avail. But he found an ally in Frank Carlucci, who met with Djukanovic and then lobbied his former understudy, Colin Powell, to consider Djkanovic's requests.

Frank Finelli—Carlyle employee.

A retired Army colonel, Finelli is perhaps the most mysterious of all Carlyle's employees. He was instrumental in working with lawmakers to push through incremental approvals of the Crusader program. He has been characterized as a "behind the scenes" type that "works in the dark."

Shafiq bin Laden—estranged half-brother of Osama bin Laden.

Shafiq is the representative to Carlyle for his family's investments with the company, and as such, was at the Carlyle annual investor conference in Washington, DC, on September 11, 2001.

Cynthia McKinney—former democratic representative from Georgia.

McKinney was an outspoken critic of Carlyle and was openly ridiculed for voicing her concerns that people close to the George W. Bush administration stood to gain financially from the ongoing war on terrorism.

Chris Ullman—Carlyle spokesperson.

Hired only after the ironies of Carlyle's bin Laden ties were discovered *after* September 11. Ullman has been a busy man, trying to hold back a barrage of negative criticism.

Paul Wolfowitz—deputy secretary of defense.

Recently profiled by the media as the man behind Bush's war fetish, Wolfowitz is also reported to be the man that killed the Crusader, not Rumsfeld. Regardless, United Defense felt no pain from the cancellation of the program when the company was awarded another contract to build a different gun the very same day.

Louis V. Gerstner Jr.—chairman of Carlyle, former IBM chief executive.

At IBM, Gerstner earned a reputation as a driven executive, directing Big Blue through an unforgettable turnaround, restoring the company's reputation as a global behemoth. It is anticipated that he will only spend 20 percent of his time on Carlyle, advising on two funds and mentoring senior managers.

PROLOGUE

MEET THE CARLYLE GROUP

A vast interlocking global network.
—Carlyle marketing material, circa 2001

It is hard to imagine a more concentrated display of wealth than Manhattan's Upper East Side, where building after building reeks of money, power, and prestige. Multimillion dollar homes share Madison Avenue sidewalks with lavish galleries, ritzy boutiques, upscale nannies, and purebreds. But even against this extravagant setting, the Carlyle Hotel stands out. Its tower rises unapologetically into the sky, lording over Central Park and dominating the skyline around it. The blue-blood interior with lush carpeting and hushed tones perfectly suits its high-end clientele. It is a place for those accustomed to success and comfortable with luxury. In a city full of opulent hotels, it is among royalty.

So it is altogether fitting that the Carlyle Group would assimilate the name of this regal residence when banding together in the summer of 1987. At the time, co-founders Stephen Norris and David Rubenstein met often at the hotel on 76th Street and Madison Avenue. They wanted the name of their company to sound like old money, and the Carlyle moniker fit the bill. But little did either co-founder know, the Carlyle Group would go on to become one of the most powerful and successful private equity firms in the world, with over $13 billion under management and more political connections than the White House switchboard. In its 15 years of existence, the Carlyle Group has become the corporate embodiment of the hotel it was named after: a towering presence in a world of wealth, power, and politics.

Today, the Carlyle Group is a story of dealings inside the "Iron Triangle," the place where the world's mightiest military intersects with high-powered politics and big business. It is a company whose history includes ties to CIA cover-ups and secret arms deals, and an astounding trail of corporate cronyism. By making defense buyouts the cornerstone of its business strategy, Carlyle now finds itself the beneficiary of the largest increase in defense spending in history. Indeed the stars seem to have aligned perfectly for Carlyle, in just 15 short years. With the ascension of George W. Bush to the presidency, the White House is now full of ex-Carlyle employees, friends, and business partners. And with the newly fattened defense budget, Carlyle has been able to extract massive profits from its defense holdings, like United Defense, in the wake of the terrorist attacks on September 11, 2001. It may be tough times for America, but as Bette Midler might say, everything's coming up Carlyle.

While the company flew well under the radar screen for the first decade of its life, lately success has not come without scrutiny for the Carlyle Group. After all, it's hard to remain anonymous when your employee roster includes names like George Herbert Walker Bush, James Baker III, John Major, and Arthur Levitt. It's also difficult to avoid those pesky accusations of corporate impropriety, conflict of interest, and influence peddling when your chairman emeritus is former defense secretary Frank Carlucci, a man who has courted controversy his entire life and spent his years at Princeton University bunking with his close friend Donald Rumsfeld, the current secretary of defense. Even George W. Bush and Colin Powell put their time in with the Carlyle Group. After years of doing business with everyone from the Bushes to members of the bin Laden family, Carlyle executives have now found their fortunes being accompanied by the cries of conspiracy.

Some critics charge that the company practices nothing more than "access capitalism," trotting out big names that bring in big money. Some call it "The Ex-Presidents Club." Some worry that it is influencing domestic and foreign policy. And some, including former Georgia congresswoman Cynthia McKinney, even implied that President Bush allowed the events of September 11 to take place to enable him to dictate policy that would benefit the Carlyle Group. But no matter how deep your suspicions run, the Carlyle Group warrants close examination. That a company like the Carlyle Group even exists is testament to the irresistible temptation for ex-politicians to cash in on their time as public servants, in ways that to some seem less than scrupulous.

The Carlyle Group has established a number of firsts in America, including:

- It is the first time a former president has toiled on behalf of a defense contractor.
- It is the first time that a former president advised his son, while holding office, on foreign policy decisions that directly impacted both of their financial fortunes.
- It is the first private-equity firm of its kind to be based in Washington, DC, rather than the traditional haunts of New York, or even Chicago.
- It is the first company to assemble a cast of characters that even *X-Files* writers couldn't have dreamed up. Besides the impressive domestic roster of political heavyweights, Fidel Ramos, former president of the Philippines is a senior advisor. Park Tae-joon, former prime minister of South Korea was also a senior advisor. Former Thai Premier Anan Panya-rachun also worked for the company.

If the thought of all of these men working together outside the fishbowl of international politics makes you uneasy, you are not alone. Political watchdog groups, like the Center for Public Integrity and Judicial Watch, have long been howling over the potential for corruption at Carlyle. The company has been investigated by the FBI, excoriated by representatives, sued by political activists, and embarrassed by scandal. Yet the Carlyle machine hums along, doing what it does best: making gobs of money for investors. Watchdogs might as well be barking at the moon, because the scandal here is not what's illegal, but what's legal.

In a time when the ties between high-ranking politicians and billion-dollar businesses has the country on edge, bracing for the next corporate scandal, and waiting for the political shoe to drop, the

Carlyle Group has come to symbolize the extent to which many of these relationships continue unchecked. And when accusations of war-profiteering ring out, Carlyle is usually at the top of most people's list of guilty parties. Coincidence and circumstance only go so far in explaining the unbridled success of this company. Connections, cronyism, and cunning fill in the gaps. Far more disconcerting to the discriminating investor is the fact that Carlyle has become the model for a new generation of investment banking in which former politicians are brought in at high-level positions to butter up investors, foreign heads of state, and business partners. Why else would Los Angeles–based Metropolitan West Financial appoint Al Gore, with zero professional investment experience, its vice chairman? Investment banks are learning that the Carlyle model pays.

But it is Carlyle's particular style of investing that has raised eyebrows. Concentrating on heavily regulated industries like defense, telecommunications, energy, and health care, Carlyle is betting that it can predict future trends in government spending and policy, or influence them outright. And by hiring former secretaries of defense, ex-presidents, the former head of the Securities and Exchange Commission, and the former chairman of the Federal Communication Commission, they are in a position to do either.

Dwight D. Eisenhower, upon leaving the office of president in 1961, warned future generations against the dangers of a "military-industrial complex," and the "grave implications" of the "conjunction of an immense military establishment and a large arms industry." He went on to presciently say, "In the councils of government, we must guard against the acquisition of unwarranted influence, whether sought or unsought, by the military industrial complex. The potential for the disastrous rise of misplaced power exists and will persist. We must never let the weight of this combination endanger our liberties or democratic process."

The wisdom of these comments has clearly been lost in the 40 years since Ike left office. The first step toward turning things around is understanding how we got here. No single company can illustrate that progression better than the Carlyle Group, a business founded on a tax scheme in 1987 that has grown up to be what its own marketing literature once called "a vast interlocking global network." The company does business at the confluence of the war on terrorism and corporate responsibility. It is a world that few of us can even imagine, full of clandestine meetings, quid pro quo deals, bitter ironies, and petty jealousies. And the cast of characters includes some of the most famous and powerful men in the world. This is today's America. This is the Carlyle Group.

1

THE POLITICIAN, THE BUSINESSMAN, AND THE UNLUCKY ESKIMOS

It was a great scam.
—Stephen Norris, co-founder
Carlyle Group, May 20, 2002

Cast of Characters

Stephen Norris	Co-founder Carlyle Group.
David Rubenstein	Co-founder Carlyle Group.
Dan D'Aniello	Co-founder Carlyle Group.
William Conway	Co-founder Carlyle Group.
Frederic Malek	Former Nixon aide, close friend of George Bush Sr., and current CEO of Thayer Capital.
Jimmy Carter	Former president of the United States.
William Barr	Former attorney general and law partner of David Rubenstein.

Stephen Norris is getting excited now. Even today, recalling the events that led to the formation of the Carlyle Group, the company that would eventually come to represent Norris' legacy, gives the 53-year-old Washington dealmaker a thrill. Though they didn't know it at the time, co-founders Norris and David Rubenstein, a young staffer from the Carter administration, were embarking on the ride of a lifetime.

1

With a nose for the big deal, the cocksure Norris is, by his own admission, a difficult man to get along with. His time with the Carlyle Group, ending abruptly in January 1995, was marked by tension, competition, and conflicting egos. He is a man with casual disregard of those with whom he is conversing. His eyes flit around the room. He looks at everything but you. He talks freely, with no fear of consequence, and rarely pauses for a retort. He talks over you. Athletic, fit, handsome, and with a healthy taste for the good life, Norris speaks longingly, even boastfully, of his time with the Carlyle Group, fondly recalling his blockbuster deals with rich Saudi princes and Fortune 500 companies. He is, and always has been, a man that swings for the fences.

In late 1986, Norris, then an executive with Marriott's mergers and acquisitions group and a tax whiz, got wind of a little-known tax loophole that allowed Eskimo-owned companies in Alaska to sell their losses to profitable companies. The origin of the loophole dated back to 1971, when Alaskan natives arrived at a unique settlement with the federal government over ownership claims of Alaskan land. Typically, when Native Americans sued the U.S. government over the atrocities committed during the nation's "manifest destiny" era, the settlements revolved around land, otherwise known as reservations. The logic went that if the government could return some portion of the land they stole in claiming America for themselves, the irreparable cultural damage done to Native Americans in the process would somehow be forgotten. But the Eskimos weren't buying it. Unlike Native Americans in the lower 48 states, Alaska's natives eschewed the traditional award of land reservations. Instead, the Alaskans chose cash. Under a unique settlement, Alaskan natives were allowed to set up native-run corporations to invest and manage the money they had been awarded. In the end, the Eskimos and other native Alaskans ended up with $962 million to manage as they saw fit. They also managed to negotiate for 44 million acres of land on which to run their businesses. It was the price paid to them for decades of oppression, and they took it.

Because of some bureaucratic foot-dragging and truly unfortunate timing, the newly formed corporations missed out on Alaska's boom time in the mid-1970s. Fishing, timber, and oil, three of the local industries most companies were set up around, experienced major downturns. Many of the companies fell prey to mismanagement, investing in foolish pursuits like tire manufacturers, concrete plants, and hotels. Even though they had chosen their own fate, the owners of the companies felt they had been set up to fail. More than 180 companies had been formed out of the settlement. Only one managed to consistently turn a profit. It was a total disaster.

The companies soon found themselves facing huge losses, and limited options for turning things around. In 1983, Alaskan Senator Ted Stevens worked to save his floundering constituency by incorporating a clause in the 1984 tax bill that allowed the Alaskan-owned companies to leverage their losses by selling them to profitable companies looking for a break on their taxes. Essentially, if an Alaskan company lost $10 million in a fiscal year, they would sell the losses for $7 million in much-needed cash. The buyer would then write the losses off against its profits, getting a $10 million tax credit for just $7 million. Everyone's happy, except, of course, the government. Norris smelled money. But he needed help from someone. Someone with exceptional connections. Someone that knew everybody, including some Alaskan Eskimos.

Someone like David Rubenstein.

Rubenstein: Carlyle's Beating Heart

Ask enough people about David Rubenstein, and you start to hear the same descriptors over and over: brilliant, driven, tireless.

Norris still maintains an objective respect for Rubenstein, with whom he joined forces in 1986. Rubenstein had been toiling as a Washington, DC, lawyer for six years with the mergers and acquisitions groups at Shaw, Pittman, Potts & Trowbridge and G. William Miller & Co. when Norris came calling. Norris, who often transitions seamlessly between utterly eloquent and outright crude, calls Rubenstein "indefatigable, "indomitable," and "f**king brilliant." Rubenstein would go on to become the very heart and soul of Carlyle, driving the company forward through clashing egos and countless near-scandals.

After graduating from the University of Chicago Law School in 1973, Rubenstein worked his way up the political ranks with blazing speed. At the tender age of 27, he became the deputy domestic policy assistant to President Jimmy Carter. He was the first person in the office in the morning, and the last to leave. One of the most widely circulated stories about Rubenstein is that he survived solely on vending machine fare during his time at the White House, a claim he does not refute. He strongly believed in the nobility of being a public servant. He was young, idealistic, and most of all, innocent.

In the spring of 1980, Rubenstein filed a memo to the president late one night. Before he left to go home—some thought that he was actually living in the White House due to his late hours—he remembered something he had intended to add to the memo, and went into the president's office to fetch the document. After shuffling through some papers in the president's inbox, he found the memo, amended it, and returned it to the stack. The next morning, President Carter questioned Rubenstein about his late-night foray into his office, asking him pointedly and repeatedly what he had seen while he was there. Rubenstein truthfully told the president that he simply got his memo, and then returned it, seeing nothing in the process. As it turns out, atop the stack of papers on Carter's desk, were the plans for the ill-fated rescue attempt of America's Iranian hostages in April 1980. The story, related to me by Norris, demonstrates Rubenstein's early naiveté. It also foreshadows the paranoia that some say has grown inside him over the past 20 years in Washington, DC. "He sees conspiracies," says Norris.

After Carter lost to Reagan in 1981, Rubenstein was released into the world of high-priced beltway lobbyists. It was a business that insulted Rubenstein's renowned intelligence and underutilized his many talents. His distaste for the work was captured in a 1993 article in *New Republic,* where he was quoted as saying, "I found it demeaning, it was legalized bribery." His opinion of lobbying would change later in his career.

Rubenstein would soon be delivered from the tedium of Washington influence peddling, when Norris, while still working for Marriott, contacted him, looking for a way to cash in on what would come to be known within Carlyle as the Great Eskimo Tax Scam.

Norris' entire job at the time was to scour tax law and find ways to save Marriott millions. He hired Rubenstein and William Barr, the man who would go on to become attorney general from 1991 to 1993, from Shaw, Pittman, Potts & Trowbridge, a Washington law firm that had represented Marriott on the Hill in the past. Along with his relentless work ethic, Rubenstein had also garnered a reputation for his extensive Rolodex. When Norris asked him if he knew any native Alaskans, Rubenstein had no problem coming up with some names.

Marriott ended up paying Rubenstein and Barr a seven-figure fee for their help in saving them a bundle on their taxes in 1986. Norris, after reading the tax bill closely, decided there was a much greater opportunity here than just this one-shot deal. He figured if Rubenstein and Barr could make out so handsomely for their limited role in facilitating Marriott's tax relief, he could, too. Norris left Marriott and set up shop in Seattle to pursue the deals, all the while talking to investors about opening up a little business of his own.

Before long, Norris and Rubenstein were flying Eskimos into Washington, DC, buttering them up, and brokering deals between them and profitable American companies. Finding the loss-making Eskimos was easier than either of them had imagined, and the profitable counterparts couldn't get enough of the free money. Norris and Rubenstein took a 1 percent cut of the transactions and sent an estimated $1 billion through the loophole. A cottage industry had been born. After clearing close to $10 million, Norris and Rubenstein recognized the ongoing potential of the business, and decided to incorporate. For corporate representation, the two hired none other than Ron Astin of the venerable Houston law firm Vinson & Elkins. (Astin would later find himself testifying before Congress about offshore partnerships he had helped set up for Enron.) With the crew in place, liabilities limited, and money coming in the door, the boys were ready to make something of themselves. All they needed now was a name.

During this time, Norris and Rubenstein frequented the Carlyle Hotel in New York. Norris loved the place. It was the kind of over-the-top lavishness he couldn't get enough of. It had a high-roller feel to it. His hero, Andre Meyer, the legendary head of investment bank Lazard Freres, had lived there for years. Norris felt the name lent the company a silk-stocking air. After selling Rubenstein on the idea, the Carlyle Group was born.

That the Carlyle Group was formed out of a temporary tax loophole, which was eliminated a year later, is utterly appropriate. David Rubenstein, as dedicated a public servant as there ever was, saw fit to found his company on a scheme that denied the federal government close to $1 billion in taxes. It was the first of many ironies that would compromise Rubenstein's political roots as his career with Carlyle progressed. As with many of the Carlyle Group's future deals, the Great Eskimo Tax Scam was entirely legal. Whether it was ethical, is another question.

The tax loophole unwittingly encouraged Eskimo companies to overstate their losses, and the IRS was called in to investigate. A discrepancy between "hard" and "soft" losses arose. Corporate appraisers took liberties in estimating the loss in value of certain goods, like timber and oil. Suddenly everyone in Alaska had losses for sale. It was a bonanza for accountants. Though no charges were ever filed, the case portends the current corporate malfeasance in America, in which companies inflate revenues and earnings through marginally legal accounting.

It bears mentioning that in certain cases, the tax loophole actually did what it was intended to do. Some Alaskan companies took the capital they received and reinvested, saving themselves from certain bankruptcy. Finally, however, just before Carlyle could complete a $500 million deal with a company called Cook Inlet, the government had seen enough of its money wasted, and sewed up the hole. It was the end of a great scheme for Carlyle, and it would be the last easy money the company saw for half a decade.

Goin' Legit

After the tax loophole closed, Norris and Rubenstein briskly went about building an empire. They brought Dan D'Aniello over from Marriott, whose salary Norris personally guaranteed. They also signed up William Conway, a former chief financial officer at MCI Communications. Funding for what Rubenstein was pitching as a leveraged buy-out firm came mainly from Pittsburgh's wealthy Richard K. Mellon family and Ed Mathias at T. Rowe Price, the Baltimore-based investment bank. It only took $5 million to get them on their way.

It was the go-go 1980s, and big business was flying high. Leveraged buyouts were the name of the game. This particular brand of cut-throat business consisted of big banks borrowing billions, acquiring huge positions in struggling companies, snatching them up on the cheap, and selling them off for parts or turning them around. Everyone was getting rich and Rubenstein was itching to get a piece of the action. He would later confess to a reporter that "I thought I had a pretty good IQ myself, and people were making a lot more money than me who I thought maybe weren't so smart."

The most important thing for buyout firms, otherwise known as private equity firms, is raising capital. The more money a given firm can raise, the more successful it can be. Like a mutual fund, a buyout fund collects money from a number of sources—wealthy individuals, institutional investors, pension funds—then invests it on their behalf. But instead of investing in stocks, buyout funds buy companies, with the intention of turning them around and selling them for a profit. Typically, the companies are bought with a mix of capital and debt, somewhat mitigating the risk of the buyer. Hence, the leveraged buyout, or LBO, nickname. The companies are then held in a portfolio, or fund, which usually has a target market or theme. It can be a dangerous form of investing, open only to the extremely wealthy. Minimum investments in a given fund are usually no less than $1 million, and returns are generally expected to be more than 25 percent, usually within 10 years, sometimes less. Downside can be that much and more. LBOs are not for the faint of heart.

The Carlyle Group based themselves in Washington, DC, instead of the more traditional buy-out firm haunts of New York or Chicago, a move that surprised many in the business. Arthur Miltenberger, then chief investment officer of the Mellon Foundation, would tell *Forbes* at the time, "I was intrigued by a merchant bank based in Washington, DC, because foreigners have to come to Washington." Upon incorporation, Carlyle hardly registered a blip on the radar of older, more established buyout firms like Kohlberg Kravis & Roberts and Fortsmann Little.

It was clear from the outset that what the Carlyle Group had to offer that was different from its more incumbent competitors was its access. Newspapers heralded the rise of a new breed of dealmaker: the access capitalist. Indeed, the Carlyle Group's first deals reflected the relationships that its founders had fostered. Carlyle took a $35 million stake in Consolidated Entertainment, a company that was part-owned by Gerald M. Rafshoon, a former Carter administration advisor. The company was planning a six-hour miniseries for HBO called "The Great Satan," a detailed account of Ayatollah Khomeini and the Iranian hostage crisis, a topic that Rubenstein knew all to well. But it soon became apparent that it takes more to succeed in the world of high finance than a political pedigree and a bunch of swell friends.

The company stumbled its way to a disastrous early record, overpaying for ill-advised investments, and getting beat out by more nimble competitors on the only deals that had potential. In 1987, Carlyle launched a takeover bid of the Mexican restaurant chain Chi-Chi's, only to be outbid by Foodmaker. Then again in 1988, Carlyle began accumulating shares of Fairchild Industries, a Virginia-based defense contractor, only to be out-bid by Banner Industries, which up until that point had been in partnership with Carlyle. It was a bruising introduction to the world of high finance. Though the company made about $10 million in stock profits on both deals combined, they were discovering the hard way how the leveraged buyout game was played.

Counting the Jews

Then in September 1988, the Carlyle Group would get an infusion of experience, and controversy, when Frederic V. Malek, a former personnel chief for President Nixon, signed on. Malek, nicknamed "The Ax" for his days as Nixon's strongman, managed

Norris and D'Aniello at Marriott in the early 1980s. Close friends with George H. W. Bush, Malek had just been rewarded for coordinating Bush's New Orleans convention with a position as deputy chairman of the Republican National Committee (RNC) in August 1988. But the excitement was to be short-lived. Less than a month after Malek's appointment, scandal erupted in Washington.

In early September 1988, the *Washington Post* reported that in July 1971, operating under instructions from President Nixon, Malek had compiled figures on the number of Jews working within the Bureau of Labor and Statistics (BLS). Nixon, then at the height of his paranoia, believed that a "Jewish cabal" within the Bureau was undermining him, releasing unfavorable and inaccurate data to the public to damage his approval ratings. Malek, in a memo dated July 27, 1971, reported that 13 of the top 35 BLS officials were indeed Jewish, and provided their names to Nixon. In the months following, Chief Economist Peter Henle and Director of Current Employee Analysis Harold Goldstein were reassigned to lower level positions within the BLS. At the time these events occurred, nothing was known of Nixon's anti-Semitic sentiments. It wasn't until 17 years later that the incident came back to haunt Malek, when *Washington Post* reporters uncovered the fateful memo while digging through old files from the Nixon administration.

After the news broke, Malek resigned as RNC chairman immediately and admitted to compiling the figures for the president, but not for reassigning the two prominent Jews. The damage had been done though. Malek knew that he would be labeled an anti-Semite. He knew the public had no tolerance for that kind of ethnically fueled politicking. He knew that he was in danger and he knew immediately where to go.

Norris called Malek the day the news hit the papers, and told him to calm down, and come over to the Carlyle offices on Pennsylvania Avenue. Malek had his motorcade sneak into the garage, so as not to be seen by anyone. "I've never seen a man so upset in my life," Norris recalls. "He was literally shaking." Norris set Malek up with an office adjoining his own, and Carlyle gave him a draw, or a salary, which Malek would theoretically have to earn back. Malek was by far the best connected of the nascent company. He brought with him deep relationships with the Bush family, the Saudi Arabian royal family, and countless Washington insiders. Even with his freshly tainted reputation, he would go on to spearhead several big deals for the company, including an ill-fated buyout of Caterair, the Texas-based airline catering company that would hire George W. Bush. Though Malek's stay at Carlyle would amount to nothing more than time on the lam, hiding out while the furor over his anti-Semitic actions died down, he did manage to set Carlyle up with a handful of high-powered Republican connections. He would soon return to public life to lead President George H. W. Bush's reelection campaign in 1991. But after Bush lost to William Jefferson Clinton, Malek found that he was no longer welcome at Carlyle. "No one wanted him back, and it was very embarrassing for Fred not to have a place to land," says Norris. "And it was wrong." Malek still harbors resentment over what he feels was mistreatment. "His wife still hates me," says Norris.

Though brief, Malek's time with Carlyle would ultimately change the face of the company forever. "I brought a little more name recognition, a little more gray hair," recalled Malek in an interview for this book. He is quick to point out that he never joined the firm outright. "I was officing there, just a freelancer," he says. In the fall of 1988, Malek brought Carlyle in on yet another ill-conceived deal to acquire Coldwell Banker Commercial, the biggest commercial real estate broker in the United States at the time. To this day, he asserts his independence from Carlyle on that deal. "It was my deal, my capital, and they just participated in it," says Malek. This exclusive attitude toward Carlyle would eventually cause enough tension between Malek and Rubenstein, that

Carlyle didn't see the need to welcome him back after Bush lost the election. Rubenstein and Conway would often refer to Malek as a "self-centered freeloader." But it was Malek who demonstrated the power of political contacts in deal making, a lesson the boys at Carlyle would take very much to heart.

Ultimately, the Coldwell deal was a bust when the real estate market did not cash in on Japanese investments as was anticipated. About the same time, Malek was helping a well-known Texas native by the name of George W. Bush, the son of then President George Bush Sr., buy the Texas Rangers major league baseball franchise. Like other deals that Malek worked while he was "officing" at Carlyle, the same people who had brought Malek in from the cold found themselves excluded from the negotiations on the Rangers.

There was one deal that Malek would let Carlyle in on, however, that both parties wish had never happened. In a classic LBO, and one of the last major deals of the booming 1980s, Carlyle would facilitate a management-led buyout of Marriott's In-Flite airline catering business. The company would later go on to be nicknamed "Craterair" by Wall Street analysts, and would remain a black mark on Carlyle's record until the mid-1990s. Though the deal would be a major bust, it wasn't all bad. It would introduce the foundering company to a young Texas businessman known simply by his middle initial: W.

2

CRATERAIR

Coffee, tea, or bankruptcy?
—*Forbes,* September 26, 1994

Cast of Characters

J. W. Marriott   Chairman of Marriott Corp., former boss to Stephen
                     Norris, Fred Malek, and Dan Altobello.

Dan Altobello   Former chairman of Caterair.

George W. Bush President of the United States of America.

Stephen Norris

Fred Malek

To understand how Carlyle works today, it is crucial to be fully acquainted with the company's long and sordid history. Each deal
the Carlyle Group made, be it a wild success or tragic failure,
helped shape what the company has become. Some buyouts that
Carlyle participated in helped them gain a better understanding
of a new industry. Some introduced them to new people—the
human collateral that would open up future opportunities. In engineering the Caterair deal, Fred Malek would accomplish both.

In the case of the Caterair buyout, Carlyle made up for the
money they lost—like many of the company's early deals, Caterair
was horrendously unsuccessful—by hiring the man that would
eventually be the leader of the most powerful country in the
world: George W. Bush. Caterair may have been a complete failure

by ordinary business standards, but the relationships cultivated therein were more than worth the stinging financial losses. In Washington, it's not what you know, but who you know, and knowing George W. Bush, then son of the nation's president, was a valuable connection indeed. But getting an in with the president's son wasn't easy, and it all started when the man known simply as "Mr. Marriott" got a hankering to sell one of his businesses.

J. W. Marriott is among the most highly regarded businessmen in the world. He has a proven track record of deft management and strong leadership. His former employees, years after they've left the company, continue to refer to him as "Mr. Marriott," out of sheer respect. He has been known to sense trends in the industry with uncanny prescience. So in 1989, when Mr. Marriott made it known that his company's airline catering division, then known as Marriott In-Flite Services, was on the block, one had to suspect that he knew something the rest of the world didn't know. Nevertheless, a group of zealous Marriott executives went ahead with plans to buy the stagnating division from Marriott Corp. with the help of the newest merchant bank on the block: Carlyle Group.

Originally formed in 1937, Marriott In-Flite had ceased to be a growth area for Marriott by the late 1980s, and Mr. Marriott wanted out. Dan Altobello, who headed the division within Marriott since 1982, decided that he would spearhead a management-led leveraged buyout of In-Flite, meaning the current employees of the division would raise the capital necessary to buy the business from Marriott. Altobello knew exactly who to call to structure the deal. In fact, he knew them quite well.

Norris, Malek, and D'Aniello, were all former Marriott executives and former co-workers of Altobello's, and together they all got to work immediately on putting together a deal. Norris' role was to work the deal such that Marriott's tax liabilities were limited. Malek was needed to help Altobello manage the new independent company (this was a special request of Mr. Marriott).

D'Aniello managed the relationship with Merrill Lynch, which would provide a $250 million bridge loan to complete the deal, the last such deal Merrill Lynch would ever partake in. Negotiations progressed, capital was raised, and then, $650 million later, in July 1989, Marriott In-Flite was sold to its employees and renamed Caterair. Carlyle retained a stake in the new company, as well as collecting a fee for structuring the deal. It would be the last major LBO of the 1980s, the decade of LBOs.

Caterair consisted of 150 different airline customers at 45 U.S. and 38 foreign airports. It had an army of 19,000 employees and revenues of $800 million in 1988. It was a very big deal. Malek and Altobello became co-chairmen and greeted the press with promises of expansion in international markets, particularly the Soviet bloc. But it was not to be.

Malek's Triangle Trade

At the same time he was working to complete the Caterair deal, Fred Malek was also putting together the largest buyout ever in the airline industry: a $3.65 billion buyout of Northwest Airlines, then the country's fourth largest carrier. Malek worked with Al Checchi and Gary Wilson, two more former Marriott executives, to buy out Northwest, and in June 1989, just days before the Caterair deal was finalized, Malek had successfully completed the Northwest deal. That Malek was working on two colossal deals simultaneously was disconcerting to the boys at Carlyle, particularly when they had cut out of the Northwest deal entirely. Just a year removed from his disgraceful exit from public life on the Bush campaign trail, and Malek had multiple irons in the fire. (He was also helping George W. Bush to buy the Texas Rangers at this time.) Controversy had slowed down Malek's political ambitions, but it did nothing to hinder his business pursuits. By October 1989, Malek had been named president and CEO of Northwest. The job required that Malek assume responsibility for day-to-day operations at Northwest, meaning he could no longer devote the time necessary to Caterair, and the burden of running the company fell solely to Altobello.

But Malek was no fool. Though he was constantly distracted by his myriad responsibilities, he still had time to make some critical moves for Caterair. By 1990, Malek had decided that George W. Bush would make an excellent board member for Caterair. "I began spending all my time on the Northwest deal, and when we did the Caterair deal, I thought he (George W. Bush) would be a good guy to be on that board," Malek told me. "His office had been next to mine on [his father's] campaign, so I knew him real well. He was coming to Washington a lot anyway, and I thought he had a lot of business judgment and practical sense. I just thought he would be a good director." George W. Bush became a board member of Caterair in 1990, the year after the company was bought out. Up to that point, Bush had a decade's worth of experience in the oil industry, but nothing even resembling the service-oriented business of airline catering. But George W. Bush had far more valuable things to offer than direct business experience. His father was president of the United States at the time and one would think that had to be worth something, both to Malek personally and to Carlyle.

In effect what Malek had constructed was his own personal triangle trade. Caterair did a sizeable business with Northwest. Northwest needed some help from the Bush administration on some regulatory issues, after Congress began questioning the airline's near-monopoly status at certain hubs. Finally, George W. Bush needed to bolster his business resume, and Malek of course was close friends with his father. Between currying favor with the president and securing business for Caterair, Malek had killed two birds with one Bush. And that's how cronyism works.

Despite Malek's public statements about Bush being appointed because of his business acumen, one Caterair board member said the real reason that Bush was named to the board was to help

Malek out on with the regulatory issues he was facing at North-west. The board member also says that Malek, Bush, and Alto-bello would often huddle together at Caterair board meetings, excluding the rest of the board. Bush's involvement in the day-to-day activities of Caterair was nominal at best. "We all coveted his custom Texas Ranger's boots, signed by Nolan Ryan," says the board member, recalling what George W. Bush added to the board. "He was really smart but not really engaged in Caterair's business." The point at which arrangements like Caterair's break down is when the few individuals who control the company are maneuvering so feverishly for their own personal gain, that the well-being of a company, and its 19,000 employees, is overlooked.

Business went on that way for a time until the airline catering industry hit a wall that Caterair was ill prepared to climb. War in the Gulf, higher oil prices, and a nationwide recession combined to devastate revenues in the airline industry. Airlines started shutting their doors, facing bankruptcy. In 1991, alone, Caterair lost two of its best customers when both Pan Am and Eastern Air Lines stopped flying because of financial insolvency.

Adding to Caterair's woes, airlines started aggressively cutting costs, and one of the first places they looked was their meal budget. By 1993, the nine major airlines had cut food costs by 8 percent. Peanuts and crackers took the place of hot meals. Low-cost airlines that rarely served meals at all, like Southwest, steadily gained popularity. The pullback vanquished profitability in the catering business, which was already operating on razor-thin mar-gins. "They could not cut costs fast enough," Malek bitterly recalls of the airlines.

Norris' Self-Destruction

Caterair lost $185 million in fiscal 1993, down from a profit of $52 million the year before, and the company was in a dire posi-tion. At this point, dissension began to fester in the boardroom.

Norris wasn't making any friends at Caterair, riding management and looking for alternatives and exit strategies for the company's quickly evaporating business. He began taking matters into his own hands, looking for buyers and raising money from personal acquaintances. He even held meetings with potential acquirers, like Sodexho, a massive international facilities management company. Norris was pushing his own agenda, and his fellow board members didn't appreciate it. But they all had their own agendas as well. With so much disparate intent in the boardroom, it's no wonder the company failed.

Then Norris went too far. Carlyle had been attempting to negotiate a management fee at Caterair, a customary payment in a leveraged buyout, but something that Carlyle did not ask for until years after the deal had been done. The Caterair board was about to approve the fee, which would at least bring some dividends from the deal back to Carlyle. To do so, the board held a meeting to vote on it. When it came time to vote, the board asked those members of the board who were also on staff at Carlyle to leave the room, due to their obvious conflict of interests. Norris, who had been attending the meeting from Paris via speakerphone, unleashed an inexplicable tirade of obscenities aimed at the board, according to people who were in the room. Apparently indignant at having to hang up during the vote, a perfectly reasonable request, Norris refused. His fiery outburst incensed the other board members, and ended up costing Carlyle the management fee. Reminded of the incident, one Carlyle staffer explained Norris' actions like this: "That's just Steve. One minute he's a brilliant businessman, on the trail of a big deal. The next he's a maniac. Steve is incredibly erratic."

Norris then instructed one of his staffers at Carlyle to work up some numbers on how a sale to Sodexho might save the equity in Caterair. Norris had very little confidence in Altobello's ability to steer the company through these troubled waters. He felt that Altobello had already missed opportunities to exit the business with their reputations and their bank accounts intact. Norris often criticized Altobello's ineptitude to colleagues and friends. So instead of bringing the paperwork to the company's CEO, he naively brought it to Malek, thinking he could confide in him. It didn't take long for Altobello to find out what was going on behind his back, and he went ballistic, according to Norris. Altobello told Norris he had no right to attempt a sale of "his" company. Norris was asked to leave the board, and it would signal the beginning of the end of his Carlyle career. But it would get even uglier.

Shortly after Norris left, in 1994, George W. Bush would also jump ship. In a move that would dog him throughout his Texas gubernatorial campaign, Bush quit the board in May, in the midst of Caterair's financial unraveling. Incumbent Governor Ann Richards attacked Bush's business record, questioning Bush's claims that he was a successful businessman. "Mr. Bush continues to insist that he's a successful businessman, but when you take a hard look at his record, it's clear that he's not what he says he is," said Chuck McDonald, Governor Richards' spokesperson. With layoffs and losses mounting at Caterair, it was hard to argue. Bush responded feebly in the *Dallas Morning News,* saying simply that "the airline food business is going from hot meals to peanuts, and this company is in the process of adjusting."

The roof was caving in fast now, the result of squabbling in the boardroom and difficult economic circumstances. *Forbes* ran a scathing expose of the company in September 1994, entitled "Coffee, tea, or bankruptcy?" In it, the magazine ridiculed Altobello for drawing more than half a million dollars in annual salary as his company went belly up. Competitors were beating Caterair to international markets, which were the only markets growing at this point. Finally, Caterair was unable to diversify into a number of the ancillary markets its competitors were exploring, because of a noncompete clause with Marriott the managers signed when they led the buyout five years earlier. It was now all too clear why

Mr. Marriott couldn't wait to unload the catering business. It was a lemon.

Adding injury to insult, Representative Harold Ford told newspapers that he nearly choked to death during a Northwest flight in 1992, catered by Caterair. The Democratic congressman from Tennessee claimed there were multiple unidentified objects in his steak and potatoes that tore up his mouth and throat. He filed a lawsuit for $18 million against Caterair. It was horribly embarrassing for the faltering company, and it would coincide with Caterair's last gasp.

In September 1995, Caterair completed a deal with Onex Food Services, the parent company of Sky Chefs, Inc. The value of the transaction was slightly more than $500 million, far less than the $650 million that was originally paid for the company, which had grown its operations in the six years it had been independent, and should have been worth much, much more. It was, by all accounts, a disastrous deal. Carlyle, Malek, and Altobello had all taken a bath on it.

By this time, Malek had been spurned by Carlyle upon his return from the unsuccessful Bush reelection campaign and had gone on to start up his own private equity concern—Thayer Capital. He offers this understated comment on Caterair's ruination: "What went wrong is that you had the Iraqi invasion of Kuwait and the explosion of oil prices, which led to reduced travel and higher oil prices for airlines. There was lower passenger count because people were afraid to travel, and now higher costs because of the huge spike in fuel. We were in a survival mode as the airlines uniformly and drastically cut food service. We had to find a way to come out of that as best we could, and we were able to do that by merging it into Sky Chefs. We got enough cash to pay off debts, and a little bit of equity. It was not a screaming home run."

The saga of Caterair serves as a microcosm of Carlyle's early years. The infighting, egos, petty jealousies, and conflicting agendas of the Caterair board were the same problems that Carlyle would wrestle with for years. Until Norris left the company in 1995, Carlyle would struggle with achieving solidarity among its upper management and creating a unified identity. Caterair was the first of many examples of the fracturing within Carlyle in the first seven years of its existence. But Caterair wasn't all bad.

Caterair turned out to be a very expensive introduction to then-President Bush's son for Carlyle. From George W. Bush, to James Baker, to George H. W. Bush, the connections made through Caterair would bolster Carlyle's ability to hook high-profile politicians leaving office. In the end, they had Malek, the man to whom they coldly turned their backs, to thank for it.

But it wasn't until 1989, after the Reagan administration had cleared out its desks, that Malek's stamp was permanently impressed on Carlyle. Rubenstein asked Malek who he thought would be a good person to hire coming out of the Reagan White House. Malek thought immediately of Frank Carlucci, the outgoing secretary of defense, and the man who had succeeded him as deputy director of the Office of Management and Budget in 1972. Malek held a cocktail party at his house in Washington, spoke to Carlucci, and quickly sealed the deal. On January 26, Frank Carlucci became vice chairman of the Carlyle Group, and life at the young merchant bank would never be the same again.

3

MR. CLEAN

They used to call him "Spooky Frank Carlucci."

—Former Carlyle employee, July 2002

Cast of Characters

Frank Carlucci	Lifelong public servant, former secretary of defense, former deputy director of the CIA.
Patrice Lumumba	Former president of Zaire, assassinated after only two months in power.
Mobuto Sese Seko	Chosen by Americans to succeed Lumumba, led Zaire into decades of famine and war.
Donald Rumsfeld	Secretary of defense, former college roommate of Frank Carlucci.
Raoul Peck	Filmmaker.
Caspar Weinberger	Former secretary of defense, Carlucci's mentor.
Roderick Hills	Former CEO of Sears World Trade.

The hiring of Frank C. Carlucci brought more than just the instant name recognition of one of the most dedicated public servants of the last three decades. It brought baggage—boatloads of baggage. Over time, the pattern of Carlyle's hiring practices emerges to reveal a series of old friends helping one another out. Norris helps out Malek, who brings in Carlucci, who helps land James Baker III, who places a call to George Bush Sr. Each successive hire helped co-founders Rubenstein and Norris climb the political ladder, which ultimately delivered Carlyle to its riches. But it was Carlucci that served as the foundation of Carlyle's political reputation. He was the first high-profile, well-publicized hire by Carlyle (Malek was kept quiet for fear of bad press). It was Carlucci that really got the ball rolling, despite his checkered past.

Depending on your political leanings, Carlucci's early curriculum vitae read either like a resume for president of the United States or a checklist of foreign policy snafus. From his days with the U.S. State Department in the explosive Congo to his clean up of the Iran-Contra affair, Carlucci has been everywhere, seen everything, and knows everyone. He has been called "Mr. Clean" for his ability to mop up politically damaging situations, and "Carlucci the Cutter," for his relentless budget trimming. It was this type of ultimate Washington insider that Carlyle was fishing for when they hooked him in the winter of 1989. And that's exactly what they got. Carlucci's tenure at the firm would result in an astonishing litany of high-powered hirings, from James Baker III to John Major to George H. W. Bush, himself. But it was Carlucci's dark political past, and the relationships fostered therein, that suddenly made Carlyle's future so bright.

Born in Scranton, Pennsylvania, in 1930 to the son of an immigrant stonecutter from Southern Italy, the diminutive, soft-spoken Carlucci attended Princeton University, where he roomed, wrestled, and recreated with close friend Donald Rumsfeld. He served two years in the U.S. Navy, took some classes at Harvard Business School, and signed up with the State Department as a Foreign Service officer in 1956. After two years as vice consul and economic officer to Johannesburg, South Africa, Carlucci was assigned to the volatile Congo (now known as Zaire) as second secretary in the U.S. Embassy. He was 30 years old.

The year was 1960, and the Congo was a dangerous place to be. The former Belgian colony received its independence in late June and was holding its first public election. But the mood was still uncertain, and the population was volatile. By July, Patrice

Lumumba and his nationalist party had assumed control of the sprawling country. Lumumba was rumored to be tight with communist factions in the Soviet Union, and the election results put the United States on edge. Even after Congo's new leadership had been established by democratic means, sporadic violence throughout the country was not uncommon.

While negotiating through tribal violence, which had been fomented by the Belgian colonial government for years, Carlucci's daughter was threatened at bayonet-point, and Carlucci himself was stabbed between the shoulder blades and arrested after a car he was riding in struck and killed a bicyclist. But Carlucci, who was once called "a tough little monkey" by his father, stayed on in the Congo, despite the life-threatening circumstances. Lumumba stayed in power only two months, replaced by Mobuto Sese Seko, America's handpicked successor, in the fall. But the threat of a Lumumba-led coup to recapture power remained. Uncomfortable with that prospect, the United States began planning an assassination attempt. A poisons expert was dispatched to the region to carry out the mission. An investigative committee led by Senator Frank Church would later reveal that President Eisenhower himself had ordered the assassination. Though many Americans suspected that their government engaged in this kind of murderous behavior during the Cold War, the Church report made it frighteningly real. And undeniably true.

Lumumba was eventually assassinated, though not by U.S. forces. Instead, rival factions within the Congo took his life during a scheduled prisoner transfer. Many still believe the United States was behind the assassination, sharing information on the time and place of the transfer with the executioners. The Church report ultimately cleared the CIA of involvement. That didn't stop filmmaker Raoul Peck, a native of the Congo who has dedicated his professional life to researching and telling the story of Patrice Lumumba, from including a scene in his docudrama *Lumumba* that shows a group of men plotting Lumumba's murder.

At one point during a vote on the means of assassination, an actor playing Carlucci is asked what he thinks. His response, intended to appear disingenuous, is, "My country's government is not in the habit of meddling in the democratic affairs of a sovereign nation. We'll respect your decision." Peck says his extensive research uncovered that Carlucci was involved in the plot at the highest level, and the scene was used to illustrate that point.

Carlucci would fight the filmmaker, and eventually have the scene edited (his name is bleeped out), saying it was a simple case of mistaken identity. "I was never as fat as that guy," he charmingly told reporters at the film's opening. "The scene is tendentious, false, libelous; it never happened, and it is a cheap shot." Peck says today that the film's distributor did not want to run the risk of a lawsuit, but Peck stands by the veracity of the film, and in particular, that scene.

Cold War Operative to Career Politician

Thus, began Frank Carlucci's rise through the ranks of the executive branch. Before being offered the number two job at the Office of Economic Opportunity (OEO) in 1969 under his old friend Donald Rumsfeld, he was accused of leading the overthrow of Joao Goulart in Brazil in 1964, Abeid Karume of Zanzibar in 1972, and Salvador Allende of Chile in 1973, according to the London *Times*. He was also accused by Italian communists of being behind the 1978 kidnapping of Aldo Moro, and subverting the revolutionary process in Portugal. "He has been a specialist in dirty work and coup attempts in the Third World," Ramon Meneses, spokesman for the Sandinista Front in Nicaragua would tell reporters later. Carlucci denied everything, and nothing was ever proven. But Carlucci had already earned a couple more nicknames—"Spooky Frank Carlucci," and "Creepy Carlucci"—and his reputation as a Cold War operative in charge of installing pro-Western governments throughout the world would follow him throughout his career.

Carlucci went on to succeed Rumsfeld at the OEO, then followed it up with stints at the Office of Management and Budget (OMB) (where he was succeeded by Fred Malek), Department of Health, Education, and Welfare (HEW), and finally landed as the deputy director of the CIA in 1978, under Carter's administration. During his time at the CIA, Carlucci was accused by conservative senators of weakening the agency through budget cuts, a charge that worked against him when those same senators voted against his nomination as deputy secretary of defense under Reagan (though he was ultimately approved for the job). He also pushed for legislation that limits the public's right to learn of CIA activity through Freedom of Information Act (FOIA) requests, an important tool for Americans wanting to know more about the actions of their elected officials.

By February 1981, working under Caspar Weinberger in the defense department, Carlucci was cultivating a new reputation, that of a master bureaucrat, efficient manager, and loyal citizen. He was seen as a problem fixer, dispatched to hot spots around the world to ensure a positive outcome for the United States. He had a history of attracting, then defusing, controversy. His legacy in tact, his connections extensive, Carlucci left the public life in 1982 for his first real business endeavor: world trade.

Secret Arms Deals

In what would later become a model for the Carlyle Group, Carlucci signed on to work with the newly formed Sears World Trade, a subsidiary of Sears designed to post executives around the world and compete with Japanese *sogo shosha* (trading companies). These massive companies leveraged size and extensive resources to conduct international trade, like timber in Thailand for paper in Paraguay, always buying low and selling high. Like the Carlyle Group five years later, Sears World Trade (SWT) curiously chose to base itself in Washington, DC, and hire exgovernment officials as its top executives.

Sears World Trade CEO Roderick Hills had been SEC chairman from 1975 to 1977, and knew Frank Carlucci from his time as counsel to President Gerald Ford, when Carlucci was working with Caspar Weinberger in HEW. Hills brought Carlucci on as president of Sears World Trade. Among the other former government officials that wound up at SWT were Curtis Hessler, former assistant secretary of the treasury, and Alan Woods, former deputy secretary of defense. The group had grand dreams of an international trading powerhouse. The end result was far from it.

The company hired more than 1,000 employees, which made it several times larger than comparable companies. And it lost money. A lot of money, very fast. Sears World Trade, lost $12 million in its first year. It lost $16.3 million in its second year. It racked up monstrous travel expenses en route to making precious few trades. The strategy was ill-defined, and by 1984, Hills would resign abruptly amid growing losses.

It was about this time when the press began speculating that company was a CIA cover up. It wasn't an illogical conclusion to draw. There was a conspicuous lack of deals. The numerous staff, many with political ties, in far-flung locations puzzled business analysts. The Washington, DC, address was very unusual. There was no income. And of course, Frank Carlucci was right in the middle of it all. Everything seemed to add up. But Hills dismissed the claims, telling the *Washington Post,* "People like to make fun of the fact that we hired high government officials," explains Hills. "We didn't do that."

Then in 1986, the press learned of covert arms deals that Sears World Trade had participated in over the previous three years. The news hit just as Carlucci, by then chairman of SWT, was chosen by President Reagan to head up the National Security Council, called in to replace John Poindexter, who resigned amid the furor over the Iran-Contra affair. The irony was thick. A new national security advisor, another arms scandal.

Using a subsidiary of SWT, called the International Planning and Analysis Center, Carlucci consulted on the buying and selling of anti-aircraft missiles, radar, jets, and other military equipment for the United States and Canada. IPAC was loaded with exmilitary, and also provided consulting to Third World countries. But nobody within SWT even knew about it. Donald Rumsfeld, never to be found too far from Frank Carlucci, was a member of the SWT board, and was quoted as saying, "We received periodic reports on Sears World Trade as an entire company, but I don't personally remember the arms deals." Another board member reacted with astonishment when he heard the news. "You're kidding," he candidly exclaimed. It appeared to be at least a breach of the public's trust, not to mention shareholders. For a brief time, the news looked like it would be a devastating blow to Carlucci's future ambitions in politics. At a time when he was being called up to restore credibility to the National Security Council, he was being dogged by accusations of yet another controversial covert action. But like so many times before, and in what would come to be his trademark, the Teflon-coated Carlucci miraculously sidestepped the controversy, and the story died quietly. Carlucci, a master at handling the press, quickly scuttled the potentially damaging story by pointing out that IPAC never did any consulting on "lethal weapons." That was enough to pacify the press, and just like that, Carlucci was back in public office.

Carlucci did not walk away from his time in corporate America empty handed. In fact, he made a small fortune, despite the dismal performance of Sears World Trade. In the disclosure papers he filed upon reassuming government work, he claimed his total income in 1986 was $1.2 million, which included more than

$700,000 as a termination settlement from Sears World Trade. Not bad for steering a company into bankruptcy.

A Farewell to Arms?

In the National Security Council, Carlucci was finally back in his element. He made fast friends with Congress and quickly cleaned house as Reagan's National Security Advisor. He jettisoned the dead weight. He called Senators. He kept an open office. And he hired a young Army Lt. General by the name of Colin Powell as his new deputy. In short, he was a natural. "Frank has a tremendous advantage in that he is one of the few people in Washington who gets on very, very well with both Cap [Weinberger] and Secretary Schultz," said Kenneth Adelman, director of the Arms Control and Disarmament Agency at the time. In fact, Carlucci was well liked by just about everyone, which in DC politics can be as much a liability as it is an advantage. Carlucci is a man known to get things done without screaming and yelling. Norris says of Carlucci, "Frank doesn't like confrontation; he likes people to agree with him."

In November 1987, Carlucci would succeed Caspar Weinberger as secretary of defense for the final year and a half of the Reagan administration. He would spend much of his time refining the budgeting and weapons procurement process, experience that would serve him well in his future role with Carlyle. While in office, he would set up an advance procurement system that favored long-term contracts with various purveyors of military goods. When Carlucci left the office of secretary of defense to join Carlyle, he would have special knowledge of which defense contractors would later be cashing in on the long-term procurement system he had arranged. And he would take advantage of that knowledge.

The relationships he established while in office would prove invaluable. In 14 months as secretary of defense, Carlucci would travel overseas 13 times, to Europe, the Middle East, Asia, and Africa. He was charming and diplomatic, and he gained supporters throughout the world. Everybody loved Frank.

In another of the stunning ironies of Carlucci's career, he fought hard to decrease spending and eliminate unnecessary weapons programs, angering military contractors and the armed forces in the process. Just 10 years later, he would find himself caught up in the same situation, only this time he would be siding with the contractors, fighting to keep outdated weapons programs alive in his role as chairman of Carlyle Group.

Despite his controversy-ridden past, Carlucci was thriving both in and out of the public domain. "Frank was washed clean by Cap Weinberger by selecting him, Ronald Reagan by nominating him, and the Senate by confirming him," says Norris. By the time Carlucci took his place at the Carlyle Group, he would have accumulated a history of covert operations, controversial assignments, disastrous business dealings, and a string of connections so powerful that, despite his dismal track record in business, any company would bend over backwards to get him. As it turned out, that company was the Carlyle Group.

4

CARLUCCI'S CONNECTIONS

Being connected to Carlyle sure doesn't hurt.
— Phil Odeen, chairman of TRW, August 21, 2002

Cast of Characters

Earle Williams   Former CEO of BDM, a highly successful defense consultancy.

Melvyn Paisley   Former Naval officer in charge of awarding Navy contracts.

Vicki Paisley   Melvyn's wife and employee at BDM.

Phil Odeen   Williams' successor at BDM, currently chairman of TRW.

Frank Carlucci

When a Pentagon official leaves office, there are federal restrictions that prohibit that person from working for a defense contractor for at least one year. It is known as a "cooling-off period." Designed to put enough time between active public servants and their subsequent private lives, the cooling-off period is widely regarded in Washington as a joke. It is nominal and rather ineffective. The reason it exists, however, is because of the extraordinary temptations that former Pentagon officials face both while they are in office, and the moment they leave, from the many defense contractors eager to get new business. Braddock, Dunn, McDonald (BDM) was one of those contractors. The company's history, both as a part of Carlyle's portfolio and outside of it, clearly demonstrates the secretive and sometimes surreptitious world of defense contracting—the world in which Carlyle has chosen to do business.

In addition, Pentagon officials, like all public officials, are often in a position to capitalize on policy decisions they made while in office. Carlyle's acquisition of BDM, as with many of their other deals, reflects more on Carlucci's knowledge of the system he helped create and his network of friends than the company's ability to identify a good deal. They are connections he made while acting as secretary of defense, as well as his many other government roles. They are very valuable connections. And it was Carlucci's connections that got Carlyle off its losing streak after a series of disastrous deals, when BDM turned into a bonanza.

Carlucci had accepted his position with Carlyle almost immediately after leaving office, but had only worked peripherally on defense deals. By September 1990, just 18 months after Frank Carlucci had resigned his post as defense secretary, the man who had reengineered defense spending and procurement at the Pentagon was ready to bring his expertise to bear on the industry he had shaped. Though he had already been wheeling and dealing on behalf of Carlyle with regard to other defense properties, he was now legally able to accept an official position with a defense contractor, an important distinction that would attract defense companies to Carlyle. With Carlucci "cooled off," Carlyle's defense prospects were really heating up.

Defense spending was still anemic after the end of the Cold War and before the beginning of the Gulf War, and Ford Motor Company was looking to divest its defense holdings, namely Ford Aerospace. Carlyle fought hard to buy the entire unit, but it lacked the capital, a shortcoming that would often plague the company in the early going. In the end, the fledgling company lost Ford Aerospace to Loral, a much more established player in defense. Loral bought Ford Aerospace for $715 million in cash. But thanks to Frank, Carlyle wasn't entirely cut out of the deal.

Carlucci's contacts would prove valuable early and often in his career at Carlyle. In particular, his close friendship with Earle Williams, president and chief executive of BDM International, a defense consulting subsidiary of Ford Aerospace, would deliver Carlyle with the firm's most lucrative defense buy out of the early 1990s.

BDM is one of the most successful defense consulting businesses in the history of the industry. When it was founded in 1959 in El Paso, Texas, the company was focused on doing weapons systems analysis, a geeky trade they plied mostly at offices in New Mexico. In 1962, they hired Earle Williams, a young engineer from Alabama, who over the next three decades, that included his promotion to CEO in 1972, came to embody the new spirit of the company, a hard-driving consultancy intent on expanding its business to all parts of the armed forces. In 1973, Williams and BDM put the harsh summers of Texas behind and moved to McLean, Virginia, just outside of Washington, DC, in order to be closer to the federal government with which it was now doing most of its business. He was moving them to where the money was.

It didn't take long for the company to learn the harsh lessons of doing business in Washington, when competitors stole contract after contract from under them because of tight political connections and well-timed campaign donations. It was a lesson that Williams learned the hard way, but one he would never forget.

Over the next two decades, the outspoken Williams would thoroughly insinuate himself into the DC power scene. Suddenly, Williams was everywhere on Capitol Hill, holding fund-raisers, heading civic activities, rubbing elbows with key politicians, and landing on highly coveted advisory boards. Among the close ties that Williams forged during this time was a friendship with Marcia Carlucci, the wife of Frank Carlucci. Williams' ability to work the room was a style of doing business that Carlyle would learn much from. And, as it turned out, it was highly lucrative. "I didn't think there was anything unusual with what I was doing at the time," says Williams, who retains his Alabama drawl and speaks with the ease of a man who has long since fought his most meaningful battles. "I just figured if you want to know people, you go where they are. It doesn't take a rocket scientist to figure that out."

Williams got to know Frank through Marcia Carlucci, and also through his work with the Defense Department (DOD) when Carlucci was secretary of defense. "When [Carlucci] was in the DOD, we had a V.P. that was working in the DOD that was on leave from us . . . sort of," says Williams.

Williams' relentless gripping-and-grinning eventually paid off. In 1984, Williams was appointed to the Naval Research Advisory Board, which consulted the Navy on long-term strategic planning. BDM's competitors couldn't believe it. How did this man manage to convince the secretary of the Navy to place him on an advisory board that allowed access to confidential information and Navy officials? Particularly when the bulk of BDM's business was with the Army and Air Force, not the Navy? (In 1983, BDM did just $1.9 million worth of business with the Navy, an insignificant fraction of their overall business and an unregistered blip on the Navy's massive procurement budget.) The answers would soon be forthcoming and would demonstrate just how much Williams had learned about doing business in the Beltway.

In the spring of 1983, BDM hired a little-known market researcher by the name of Vicki Paisley for a yearly salary of $40,000. It turned out to be an excellent hire. Paisley's husband, Melvyn Paisley, was in charge of awarding Navy contracts. A year after the hiring of Vicki Paisley, Williams landed the coveted position on the Navy's advisory board. "Mel was instrumental in getting me on that board," recalls Williams, who says that Paisley approached him for the position, and Williams initially demurred. "I think you've got the wrong man, we work mostly with the Air Force and the Army," Williams told Paisley. But Paisley wouldn't relent, and eventually succeeded in signing up Williams. It was a coup for Williams, and it paid off almost immediately. Between his appointment to the Naval Research Advisory Board in 1984 and the end of fiscal 1987, BDM had more than doubled its contracts with the Navy from $3.1 million to $6.6 million. Then, in the beginning of fiscal 1988, BDM was reporting to shareholders an expected $62 million in Navy contracts, according to a *Washington Post* article. The build up in Navy contracts had other defense contractors from around the world scratching their heads. Competitors accused Williams of hiring Vicki Paisley as a favor to Melvyn, who then brought in Williams to the advisory board, and subsequently awarded Navy contracts to BDM. The situation reeked of perceived impropriety, and the newspapers covered the entire story in great detail, but inexplicably no investigation was called for at the time.

Much of the new business BDM was garnering was in an area the Navy called *Black Projects,* or budgets that are kept secret because to publicize them would compromise national security. Lawmakers often complain about Black Projects, citing that many contracts are thusly classified, not because of national security concerns, but rather to avoid the required congressional review. Regardless, BDM was suddenly ratcheting up its Navy business year after year. When Melvyn Paisley left the Pentagon in 1987, he took a job alongside his wife, consulting for BDM. It was a good time to get in. The company was clearly growing fast, and in the midst of its good fortune, was bought in May 1988 by Ford Aerospace for an eye-popping $425 million. Times were good, and Earle Williams had finally showed the cutthroat defense contractors how business was done in the Beltway.

Then in the summer of 1988, Operation Ill Wind swept through the Pentagon, exposing a ring of corruption, bribery, and fraud that would eventually send dozens of officials to jail for rigging the awarding of defense contracts. For years, various elements in the government had suspected widespread corruption in the Pentagon and the defense business. Several years of covert investigation proved those suspicions true. It was a crushing blow to the credibility of the Pentagon and the secretary of defense at the time, Frank Carlucci. Arrests, arraignments, and convictions rained down weekly on the Pentagon, armed forces officials, and the defense contractors with whom they all did business.

The most prominent official convicted in the seven-year investigation was none other than Melvyn Paisley, who pleaded guilty to conspiracy to defraud the government, bribery, and theft of government property. He was sentenced to four years in prison for taking kickbacks. The FBI investigated BDM and the connection between Williams, Paisley, and his wife. Documents from the Paisley home were confiscated, including at least a dozen relating to BDM. Williams was told that he would eventually need to testify in front of the grand jury, but the bureau was unable to bring a case against BDM, and, as Williams says, "Ill Wind just blew away."

Williams had this to say about his role in the investigation: "In hindsight, I understand why people would have thought we participated [in illegal activity]. When Vicki Paisley came to see me, I didn't know who she was, but she wanted the job. I was aware of a potential conflict, and I told her that it probably wouldn't be suitable. But she said she really wanted to work for me. I asked her why she was leaving her job at Computer Sciences Corp. (CSC). She said it was because Mel told her to because CSC was doing too much Navy business, and it looked bad. I guess that's ironic. When Ill Wind hit, we started to lose business, but I told our clients we hadn't done anything wrong. There was never any real involvement of BDM in Ill Wind, and I guess the FBI just eventually figured we were small potatoes."

But the damage had been done. Between the residue left from the scandal and the end of the Cold War, the value of BDM, now a subsidiary of Ford Aerospace, plummeted. When Loral picked up Ford Aerospace in the fall of 1990, Williams was intent on not working for Bernie Schwartz, then the head of Loral, for personal reasons. Ironically, Williams convinced Schwartz that owning BDM would be a conflict of interest for Loral, since BDM had consulted the Pentagon on systems that Loral produced. The perceived conflict of interest inherent in hiring Vicki Paisley seven years prior hadn't weighed on Williams' conscience quite as much, apparently.

After Williams got in touch with his good friend Frank Carlucci, Conway negotiated the purchase, and $130 million later, BDM was the newest company in Carlyle's portfolio. That was less than a third of the $425 million Ford Aerospace had paid for the company just two years prior. Carlucci landed a job as chairman, Conway snagged a seat on the board, and Williams stayed on as president and CEO. It was a steal.

A New Friend

After a couple of years, Williams, age 62, aspired toward a career in government service and, in early 1992, announced his retirement from the $400,000-a-year CEO job at BDM. It was time for another friend of Frank. This time, Carlucci turned to an old buddy and tennis partner by the name of Phil Odeen, currently chairman of TRW. A vice chairman at Coopers Lybrand at the time, Odeen had known Carlucci for decades, having spent 13 years in the office of the secretary of defense early in his own career. Carlucci's wife had even worked with Odeen at Coopers. Odeen was also good friends with Williams, and so the circle was complete. Over a tennis match in the winter of 1992, Carlucci popped the question.

"He asked me if I had any interest in the job, and I had just been promoted to vice chairman at Coopers and moved to New

York," Odeen told me. "I said no thanks, but if you don't find the right person, give me a call." Carlucci called the very next morning and arranged a Sunday morning breakfast meeting in DC between Conway, Rubenstein, and Carlucci. Apparently, Carlucci had indeed found the right person, and it was Odeen. Within a week, Odeen had an offer, and by May, Odeen was the new president and CEO of BDM. "It all happened very fast," recalls Odeen.

Under Odeen's watch, BDM would transform itself from a business heavily reliant on defense contracting to a more diversified services company. "The Cold War was over, and defense budgets were coming down," explains Odeen. "Information and communications technology were more important than ships and tanks." Odeen did a bang-up job getting BDM into emerging enterprise resource planning (ERP) and warehouse automation markets. But it was still defense that buttered BDM's bread. And controversy in that arena was set to strike yet again.

On Christmas Eve, 1994, the *New York Times* reported that Frank Carlucci had again been involved in a clandestine arms deal, this time with the Soviets. With Carlucci as chairman, BDM, now a Carlyle portfolio company, had brokered a deal between the Pentagon and the former Soviet Republic of Belarus to secretly purchase an S-300, the Soviet's version of the Patriot missile defense system the United States had used so effectively during the Gulf War.

After the Cold War, the Russians were selling weapons to both allies and enemies of the United States. They needed the cash and no longer had much use for weapons, so the Russians opened up an arms bazaar. In another black budget project, BDM was hired in 1992 to acquire the S-300 for the Defense Intelligence Agency's Missile and Space Intelligence Center in Alabama. American forces wanted the weapons so they could take them apart, see how they work, and develop ways to defeat them.

For the deal, BDM used the infamous Canadian arms dealer Emmanuel Weigensberg, the same man that brokered the Iran-Contra arms shipments for the Reagan White House. The reason for the secrecy around the deal, says Odeen, was that the Russians were selling the same weapons to America's enemies and wouldn't want those customers to know the Russians were playing both sides of the fence. But others speculated that the Russians had been duped. That they never knew they were selling the S-300 to the Americans, and had they known, would never have gone through with the transaction. Hence, the need for a middleman like Weigensberg, to obfuscate the actual buyers. Odeen denies those accusations. "We did not do these deals openly or publicly, but they [the Russians] knew who they were selling to," says Odeen. "This was a decent business for us. We had the relationships, and we were essentially a broker."

But BDM's competitors didn't see it that way. Again, there were charges of favoritism, cronyism, and quid pro quo. Russian military officials were reportedly incensed by the transaction, claiming they had no knowledge of the ultimate buyer. Competitors griped about their inability to penetrate the relationship between BDM and the Pentagon.

They said that BDM's connections, particularly within Carlyle, were to blame. At the time, Pentagon spokesperson Kenneth Bacon told the *Times* that he was "concerned about any allegations of unfairness and will review them as appropriate." But BDM was cleared again. The company seemed to have acquired Carlucci's Houdini-esque ability to sidestep scandal.

As it turned out, BDM had in place something called a "basic ordering agreement," or an ongoing, open-ended, long-term contract with the Pentagon. The agreement did put BDM on an inside track with regards to foreign weapons procurement. "Otherwise, it can get very bureaucratic," says Odeen. As for Carlucci's potential involvement, having advocated long-term contracts that protect vendors like BDM when he was secretary of defense, Odeen recites an exculpatory mantra heard over and over again throughout Carlyle's history. "I don't think Frank had anything to do with that at all," says Odeen. He adds, "But being connected to Carlyle sure doesn't hurt."

Indeed, BDM's connections to Carlyle have done nothing but help them. And the deal didn't work out too badly for Carlyle, either. First, Carlyle took the company public in 1994. Then in 1997, TRW paid $975 million for BDM, making Carlyle's $130 million investment just seven years earlier, look brilliant. Phil Odeen went on to become the chairman at TRW, which then became one of the largest defense contractors in the country. In the words of Fred Malek, *this* deal was a "screaming home run."

Carlyle also used BDM in doing due diligence on future defense deals. It was a perfect setup. Because BDM had so much consulting experience and had worked with most of the major contractors, Carlyle had built in proprietary knowledge of dozens of defense companies. And this is where the bulk of Carlyle's early deals would come from. Some were more successful than others, but with defense, Carlyle had found a calling. They had found a business that they understood, in which they had myriad connections, and could make loads of cash. They had found what would become their identity.

But with the acquisition of BDM, Carlyle was agreeing to do business in the shadowy world of defense contracting; a murky business with which Carlucci was well acquainted, but Norris and Rubenstein knew little about. The decision to go down this road would eventually make Carlyle one of the largest defense contractors in the country and would create the controversial behemoth it is today.

5

GETTING DEFENSIVE

It's like shooting fish in a barrel.
—Former Chrysler chairman Lee Iacocca,
Washington Post, March 31, 1985

Cast of Characters

M. W. Gambill   Former CEO of defense contractor Harsco.
Norman Augustine Former CEO of defense contractor Martin Marietta.
William Conway
Frank Carlucci

Legendary former chairman of Chrysler, Lee Iacocca, had a habit of asking his contractors, many of whom also sold goods to the military, whether making money in defense was a sure thing. "They start chuckling, and they look around to see if the office is bugged," said Iacocca in an interview in the mid-1980s. "And they say, 'It's like shooting fish in a barrel.'"

No one knew this better than Frank Carlucci, who fresh off his 18-month stint as secretary of defense, was getting his feet wet in the world of high finance for the first time since his unsuccessful run with Sears World Trade. But this would be different than his earlier disasters. Carlucci was going to deal in the industry he knew best: defense. After the BDM deal was completed, the rest of the defense world knew Carlucci meant business.

In the years following the BDM acquisition, Carlyle would embark on a stunning series of defense dealings, fighting it out with the giants of defense contracting, and quite often having their hats handed to them. But many of the deals they did win were hugely successful, as well as controversial, and built them into the nation's eleventh largest defense contractor. The disconcerting pattern of doing business with questionable companies continued, however, and signaled Carlyle's willingness to dwell in the dark underworld of the defense industry. With BDM's consulting help, Carlyle made a run at the top defense players in the nation and, when it was all said and done, carved themselves a place at the top.

An Arsenal of Democracy

The government has a long history of overpaying for weapons, offering interest-free loans, waiving federal taxes, bailing out floundering defense contractors, and even paying generous termination fees to unsuccessful vendors. The Defense Department has bailed out more than 6,000 defense companies since 1958, under an act of Congress known as the Extraordinary Contractual Relief Act. It is all done in the interests of "national security." And it amounts to a government-subsidized industry, doing business over a safety net.

Carlucci had as much to do with the current state of defense spending as anybody. As deputy defense secretary under Weinberger, Carlucci developed a Pentagon policy of procurement that called for higher profits for the defense industry. It also lowered the risks within defense contracting, ensuring long-term and no-bid contracts, both moves intended to encourage private companies to enter the market. Privatization, the practice of taking government-run offices and departments and forming for-profit, private companies, was all the rage. The idea was to build up a healthy and happy private defense industry that would carry the United States to victory in the Cold War. And juice the economy while we were at it.

It worked. The defense industry blossomed under Reagan's watch by creating, and the former president himself termed it, an "arsenal of Democracy." At one point in 1985, a *Washington Post* expose on the defense industry uncovered that the Pentagon was spending an average of $28 million an hour—24 hours a day, 7 days a week. The top 13 contractors had revenues of more than $122 billion. Those same contractors were also the ones consulting the government on which weapons to buy and when. And few of the defense contractors were paying taxes. The numbers were astounding. It was a great time to be in the defense business. But it wouldn't last.

Just nine months after Carlucci took his post at Carlyle, the defense business came to a screeching halt, marked by the felling of the Berlin Wall on November 10, 1989, and the subsequent end of the Cold War. The defense industry went into instant retreat. Secretary of Defense Richard Cheney announced a "peacetime dividend" and quickly slashed $180 billion off the defense budget. Because of the end of the Cold War, everyone knew that the budget cuts were imminent, but no one thought it would be so quick, and so severe. Values of defense companies plummeted. Contractors didn't know what had hit them. It was a perfect time to get into defense buyouts, when all the properties were cheap, and Carlucci knew it.

After the BDM buyout, Carlyle began bearing down on the defense market in earnest. The first object of its affection was a Pennsylvania-based industrial company that owned an undervalued defense division that made howitzers and other military equipment, Harsco Corp. The defense division that Harsco harbored would later become the now well-known United Defense (much more on that later). The only problem was, Harsco wasn't interested in selling. Harsco employees didn't want to sell the company at such a low point, locking in their losses. As a result, they resisted Carlyle's overtures, which often happens in the fierce world of leveraged buyouts, as companies struggle to maintain their independence during hard times, while the vultures circle above.

Carlyle went to plan B. If they couldn't convince Harsco management to sell the company outright, they would start snatching up public shares. It was more time-consuming and generally more expensive to acquire a company this way, but the thinking is that by gaining a large position in stock, they could begin to exert some pressure on Harsco's management. So Carlyle began accumulating a large stock position in Harsco, about 6 percent of the total shares outstanding. If they didn't want to sell, Carlyle was going to put the screws to them, threatening to acquire a majority share in the company. Then, at 2:30 P.M. on Ground Hog Day 1990, Harsco CEO M. W. Gambill got the call from Frank Carlucci.

It is known as a courtesy call, making a CEO aware of an aggressor's increasing position in a public company, as if Gambill hadn't already noticed. Carlucci and the boys at Carlyle had their eye on Harsco's defense division, whose value had been decimated by the retreat in defense spending. But Harsco still wasn't interested. Carlyle quickly increased its position in the company, until it became the majority shareholder with nearly 7 percent of the company. It submitted a restructuring plan to the company that included a tempting $15-a-share dividend, an appeal to shareholders of the company, a move designed to outflank Harsco's management. Harsco still wouldn't budge, and the company rejected the proposal outright. It was a slap in the face to Carlyle, and symbolic of the company's early lack of clout. Carlucci's reputation alone was not enough to get potential buyout targets excited. The company had no track record, and Harsco could not be sure of its intentions. Would Carlyle just break the company up and sell it for parts? Or would they nurture it back to health, then sell it for a profit? There was no precedent by which

Harsco could judge Carlyle. And they would just as soon not do business with them.

Carlyle was not through, however. The company upped its stock position to 10 percent, and demanded two positions on Harsco's board, as negotiations became more contentious. Harsco, under significant pressure now, compromised, offering Carlyle one position on its board. But Harsco never sold the unit to Carlyle outright. Harsco had maintained its independence and fended off a hostile takeover. It cost Carlyle $63 million in stock to gain that one board seat, not to mention the time and labor costs of doing due diligence on Harsco. On the surface, it was a terrible deal. But six years later, when Carlyle used that board seat to steal United Defense away from General Dynamics, it would prove to be one of the best deals the company ever made.

More Ill Wind

Shortly after this failure, Carlyle turned its attention to another highly controversial acquisition target: Unisys Corp. Now known mostly for its mainframe computer and IT services business, Unisys was among many companies looking to divest itself of a money-losing defense division. But in June 1988, in the middle of Carlucci's tenure as defense secretary, Operation Ill Wind, the same investigation that had attempted to nail BDM, took down Unisys. The probe, led by Assistant U.S. Attorney Joseph Aronica, resulted in convictions against 45 individuals and $225 million in fines. It was a comprehensive web of corporate and political corruption in the military, exactly what Eisenhower had warned against 30 years earlier. And it was all uncovered during Carlucci's watch.

In September 1991, after the probe was complete, Unisys alone paid $190 million in fines for bribing public officials en route to hundreds of millions of dollars in contracts. The company pleaded guilty to conspiracy, bribery, and illegally overbilling the government. Unisys had been disgraced and, as a result, was thoroughly devalued. Of all the companies implicated in Operation Ill Wind, Unisys probably took the worst hit. And now, Carlyle was looking to pick the defense division up on the cheap.

Ultimately though, much like with Harsco, Carlyle would fail. Unisys and Carlyle would flirt for the better part of a year before Unisys chose to take the division public instead. Carlyle was having trouble convincing potential buyout partners to get in bed with them, an obstacle that is not uncommon for young buyout firms. Each failed takeover attempt costs money, though. And the payoffs were not forthcoming. It was another devastating setback for the incipient company, but it would not prove fatal. Not even close.

The folks at Carlyle were learning on the job. They had taken a few lumps, but in the company's 1992 bidding war for the defense and aerospace division of LTV Corp., they would show off their newly acquired erudition. The saga of LTV would ultimately consume a full year, involve multiple court battles, and even require a presidential intervention before it was done. Rubenstein would call it the most difficult transaction he had ever been involved in. It was, in a word, wild.

The fun once again started with a call from Frank Carlucci, this time to his friend Norman Augustine, chairman of defense giant Martin Marietta and former assistant secretary of the Army. Together with Lockheed Corp., Martin Marietta had announced on February 3, 1992, the purchase of LTV's defense and aerospace division, which was in bankruptcy at the time, for $355 million. It was a steal and, for all intents and purposes, a done deal. But on March 27 of that year, Augustine took a call from Carlucci, who asked if Lockheed and Martin Marietta might be willing to cut Carlyle into the deal.

Augustine was shocked and confused. For the past few months, Carlyle had been putting together a competitive bid for the division, with its partner Thomson-CSF, the French defense contractor.

Why would Carlucci be asking in on his deal? Especially now, when it was practically done?

As it turned out, things weren't going so well between Carlyle and Thomson. Carlyle once again couldn't get the financing in order for its share of the deal, and Thomson wouldn't proceed without it. The fragile partnership the two had constructed was falling apart. Thomson chairman Alain Gomez was calling around, looking for other partners that had the capital, and could complete the deal. All of which led Carlucci to call his old friend Augustine.

Bill's Will

Conway and Rubenstein met with Augustine and offered $50 million to get in, money they said would be useful if Thomson were to succeed in finding another partner and make a new more competitive bid at the eleventh hour. Augustine turned them down flatly, apparently unconvinced that Thomson would ever reemerge as a real threat. It looked like it was over. Thomson officials had abandoned hope, and Augustine felt certain that LTV was his. But Bill Conway had other ideas.

A relentless businessman, Conway was largely responsible for building MCI Communications into a major player in the telecommunications industry as chief financial officer during the 1980s. He had an impeccable reputation in financial circles, often cited as one of the top handful of CFOs in the country. He was a fearsome manager in the Carlyle offices, building tight-knit groups of his favorite employees and largely ignoring the rest of the company. One former employee said, "You're either in with Bill or your out, and if you're out, he'll make your life miserable."

Conway is a conservative businessman from New England and a real company man. Many ex-employees credit him with cultivating an atmosphere of intimidation in the Carlyle offices, putting employees in place by firing off companywide e-mails stating, "I'm sick and tired of people complaining about *their* offices and *their* office furniture. It's not *your* office or *your* furniture. It's *mine*." He was notoriously cheap and would often gripe loudly about there being too many employees at Carlyle, "sitting around *my* offices, drinking strawberry flavored water."

The way Carlyle was structured, the partners got very, very rich from big deals, and no one else saw a dime outside of their salary. Conway would inexplicably remind employees of this sore spot when he would close out a company meeting by proclaiming it was time to go out "and make me money." According to those who worked for him, he could be alternately brilliant, driven, and despotic. And he never gave up on a deal.

Two days before the bankruptcy judge was to award LTV's assets to Martin Marietta and Lockheed, Conway got the needed money together from Carlyle's old benefactor, the Mellon family, and called Thomson to make nice. With the money in hand, Thomson and Carlyle quickly resolved their differences, waltzed into bankruptcy court, and offered $400 million in cash for LTV aerospace, $45 million more than the Martin Marietta/Lockheed team had offered. Conway had pulled it off, against all odds. Augustine was floored, and defeated. Or so it seemed.

This war was just heating up. Augustine kicked it into overdrive, setting up meetings with Assistant Secretary of Defense Paul Wolfowitz, Deputy Secretary of Defense Don Atwood, and Assistant Secretary of the Army Stephen Conver. Augustine argued that selling LTV's defense and aerospace division to Thomson, a company partly owned by the French government, would be a breach of national security. Martin Marietta sent a raft of lobbyist to the Hill to persuade lawmakers to come out against the deal. And quickly the tide turned. Augustine was making progress in blocking the sale. Carlucci worked the phones, as well, getting assurances from several Pentagon officials that the deal would go through, despite the concerns of lawmakers over foreign ownership.

In the final day of bankruptcy court, the bidding escalated rapidly. Augustine had created enough uncertainty over whether the U.S. regulatory agencies would approve the deal, that the game was once again wide open. Because LTV's creditors were concerned over regulatory approval of the deal, which wouldn't be known until months after the actual sale, Carlyle and Thomson were forced to increase their bid to $430 million, plus a $17 million nonrefundable deposit. In the event that the sale was denied by lawmakers under national security concerns, Carlyle would pay LTV $17 million for nothing. Martin Marietta and Lockheed upped their bid to $385 million and urged creditors to consider the likelihood that the Carlyle-Thomson deal would never get approved. Carlyle would eventually offer another $20 million, plus a $20 million nonrefundable deposit. That was enough, and the judge awarded LTV's missile division to Thomson and the aircraft division to Carlyle. The boys from Carlyle had finally done it. They had gone up against the best, and won.

Augustine said of the decision, "Even when it's over, it ain't really over;" words that would prove to be prescient. Sure enough, the Bush administration went on record opposing the sale, and Congress voted 93–4 that selling LTV to a French company would be "detrimental to the national security interests of the United States." Despite the assurances that Carlucci had gotten from the Pentagon, the sale never really had a chance in Congress. Thomson would eventually pull out of the running altogether, flinging the door open to renewed bidding, and getting Augustine back into the game. The race was on again.

This time Carlyle teamed up with Loral Corp. and Northrop, more formidable partners than Thomson, not to mention American companies, and finally outbid the Marietta-Lockheed team with a price of $475 million. They renamed the division Vought

Aircraft and managed to turn the flailing company around. Carlyle's contribution to the sale was $38 million, a stake that the company would then sell back to Northrop Grumman for $130 million in just two years. It was a lucrative deal. And it legitimized Carlyle's band of ex-politicians in the wheeling and dealing world of defense buyouts.

Finally, Carlyle was being viewed as a player. Though still accused of practicing access capitalism and suffering a number of brutal early setbacks, the LTV deal burnished their reputation as serious competitors, willing to do whatever it takes to make a deal happen. In conjunction with the BDM deal, Carlyle now had to be taken seriously around the Beltway. But there was another deal in the works that would really put Carlyle on the map—the world map.

6

AN ARABIAN WHITE KNIGHT

*Politically, it could be considered a quid
pro quo for the United States.*
—Shafiqul Islam, senior fellow at the Council on
Foreign Relations, *Washington Post,* February 22, 1991

Cast of Characters

Prince Alwaleed bin Talal bin Abdul Aziz Al Saud	Saudi Arabian prince, billionaire, international investor.
King Fahd	King of Saudi Arabia.
Faissel Fahad	San Francisco lawyer, friend of Prince Alwaleed.
Prince Sultan bin Abdulaziz	Saudi Arabian defense minister.
Stephen Norris	

The early part of 1991 was literally an explosive time in the world. Bombs were raining down over Baghdad in the latter stages of the Gulf War. Scud missiles were careening their way past U.S. defenses in Saudi Arabia. And the savings and loan crisis had the nation's economy in full retreat. But this rare and tragic confluence of events had set up one of the best business deals of the year, and possibly the decade. A deal that would put Carlyle on the front page of newspapers around the world.

Prince Alwaleed bin Talal bin Abdul Aziz Al Saud, more economically known as Prince Alwaleed bin Talal, was 35 in 1991 and eager to invest his fortunes across the world. The nephew of Saudi Arabia's King Fahd bin Abdul Aziz Al Saud, the Prince was a glamorous, wealthy jet setter who had spent much of his formative years studying in the United States. After earning his bachelor's degree in business administration at tiny Menlo College in California in 1979, he went to Syracuse University in upstate New York to get his masters in social science. Upon returning to Saudi Arabia, the Prince immediately began building his investment portfolio, mostly in real estate and construction. At first, he wasn't so good at it, and he burned through a $30,000 gift from his father within months. At that time, he approached Citigroup in Riyadh, an American bank, to ask for a loan. They rejected him flatly. But he went on to accumulate millions, at least some of which came through acting as a liaison between foreign construction contractors and local businesses, though the source of much of the Prince's fortunes remains unknown. Through his gains, he formed the Kingdom Holding Company, an investment vehicle through which he could play with his millions. But the Prince was looking for more, much more. He was looking toward investing in America.

The timing was right. America and Saudi Arabia were cooperating on defeating Saddam Hussein's aggression in Kuwait. It was one of the first times the United States and Saudi Arabia had their political agendas in line. Saudi Arabia had committed more than a hundred thousand troops to the conflict in the gulf, and those soldiers were fighting beside American troops. Many saw this as the dawn of a new era of cooperation between the two nations, both politically and financially. And they were right.

Back at home in the United States, the mighty banks were gasping for air. Stocks were plummeting all around the financial sector, and bankruptcies were not uncommon. The fallout from the savings and loan crisis was littered along Wall Street. It was on this shaky ground that Citicorp, America's largest bank at the time, found itself in February 1991. The company's stock had collapsed, losing half its value between the summer and winter of 1990. It was in desperate need of financing, a lot of financing. Citicorp was looking for as much as $1.5 billion to stay afloat, and they were hoping to raise it through the sale of stock. They were looking for a white knight.

A Saudi Savior

Enter the Prince. Prince Alwaleed was watching the events in the United States closely, as he always did, and he had decided it was time to put his money to work in America. Known for his eccentricities, the Prince would often drag a caravan of trucks out into the desert to relax. There, with the baking, barren desert glowing all around him, he would sit in a tent complex, entertain guests, and watch multiple satellite television hook ups, staying abreast of world news. A seasoned critic of American media, he had been following the saga of Citicorp from the beginning. He decided it was time to invest.

Working through his representative in the United States, San Francisco lawyer Faissel Fahad, the Prince was put in touch with a prominent DC-based law firm. Because of the tricky political nature of a deal involving a major U.S. bank and a foreign investor, the firm felt they needed an advisor that offered more than just traditional investment banking advice. They decided they needed the Carlyle Group, to help them navigate the choppy waters of federal approval for the deal. After all, Carlyle had the government connections, they were based in DC, and a sensitive deal like this was going to need a delicate political touch. They called Norris.

The Prince had loads of cash, and Citicorp needed it. But at the time, Treasury Secretary Nicholas Brady had been pushing reform in the banking industry, to allow banks more flexibility in the types of business they could enter. It was intended to diversify banks from the disastrous savings and loan business, and strengthen the industry by giving it more options. But there was concern that opponents to the legislation would use the fear of foreign ownership in American banks as a sticking point to hold up the reform. A deal between a wealthy Saudi Prince and the nation's largest bank was all reform opponents needed to prove their case. It was, to say the least, a very sensitive time in the banking industry. Norris and the Prince knew this, and the two worked hard to structure a deal with Citicorp that would allay any and all concerns, but still get the much-needed capital into the hands of Citicorp.

Norris and the Prince spoke often, sometimes two or three times a day, for hours on end. One conversation was temporarily interrupted while the Prince watched the American Patriot Defense system shoot down an Iraqi Scud missile outside his window. Unphased by the attack, the Prince and Norris picked up the conversation where they had left off. "It was a crazy time," remembers Norris. "The Prince and I were extremely close. I have a passport full of Saudi stamps. I don't even know how many times I went over there."

The negotiations were cordial but intense. During the deal-making process, Norris asked Citicorp for a board seat in return for the Prince's investment. It was a pure red herring. A shrewd negotiating tactic, designed to be dropped in a show of concession, which it later was. Neither the Prince nor Norris thought they would get it. In fact, they knew it would make the Federal Reserve Board's approval of the deal nearly impossible. But it worked to perfection.

After months of preparation, they got the deal preapproved by the Federal Reserve Board (Fed), by conceding measures they never intended to secure and assuring members that the Prince would be a passive investor. The thinking at the Fed was that everyone wanted the Prince to invest his money to save Citicorp, they just didn't want him to exercise any control over his investment. It was a lot to ask, but Norris and the Prince had expected it. The Fed also spent months researching where the Prince's money was coming from. Rumors that Prince was acting as a front for other investors ran rampant. There was concern about Middle Eastern investors using the Prince to launder their money. But finally, the Fed relented, and the deal went through.

On February 21, 1991, a mammoth deal was announced. The Prince would be purchasing $590 million worth of stock in Citicorp, and bailing out the bank that once turned him away when he needed a loan back in his home country. The shares were nonvoting preferred stock, which meant that the Prince could not vote his shares in proxy battles. But, he would be allowed to convert the shares to common stock at an exercise price of $16 a share in just eight months. He already owned 4.9 percent of the common stock, which he had acquired over time in the fall of 1990. That meant that if he were to convert his shares in October 1991, he would hold almost 15 percent of the common shares. In other words, he would be one of the company's largest shareholders.

Media Misteps

The stock jumped up 8 percent in the week following the announcement, and the press was all over the news. Who was Prince Alwaleed? How did he get so much money? Who is the Carlyle Group? Would the Prince be seeking a board seat in return for his investment? Is this a new beginning for financial cooperation between Saudi Arabia and the United States?

There with the answers to all of these pressing questions, in all his glory, was Stephen L. Norris, the co-founder of the Carlyle Group and the man who had engineered the biggest deal of the year. He was quoted everywhere, and figured prominently in a *BusinessWeek* profile of the deal. Norris told the press that the Prince would not be asking for a board seat. But that he didn't plan to be completely passive either. After all, who invests $590 million of his own money and doesn't expect his voice to be heard on important decisions? No, Prince Alwaleed would be an "active" investor, said Norris.

Norris' statements proved to be well off the mark, and they set off the alarm bells at the Federal Reserve Board, the same board that had already been promised Alwaleed would remain a passive investor. Originally, the Fed had been assured that Alwaleed would not attempt to "influence management" for at least five years, though he would be allowed to speak his views to the board of directors, says Norris today. That was the deal. But Norris' statements to the press after the deal appeared to contradict that agreement, and the Fed wanted some answers.

The Prince's people feverishly worked the phones that next day, desperately trying to convince the Fed that Norris was out of line, not expressing himself clearly, and that the Prince had every intention to remain passive. In the middle of all of this, a 1988 article in *Forbes* surfaced, in which Alwaleed is quoted as saying the role of the passive investor is not for him. "I want my voice to be heard . . . I would love to be a corporate raider," he said. Suddenly, the whole reason that the Prince had chosen Carlyle in the first place—to help him traverse the rocky regulatory terrain—had blown up in his face.

In addition, the Prince took grave offense at what he perceived as Norris taking credit for the deal in the press. The Prince, not unreasonably, wanted to be seen as the savior of Citicorp. Instead, Carlyle was getting all the credit. Norris' Carlyle partners also felt he was becoming too personally involved in the success of a client, too public. The fiasco that resulted began the long, drawn-out process of Norris' excommunication from the firm.

Ultimately, and after much cajoling, the Fed allowed the deal to go through. But they forced the Prince to sell the 4.9 percent of common shares he had previously accumulated, and mandated that he not own more than 9.9 percent of the overall stock.

The move cost the Prince millions in future profits. It was a public sign from the Fed that they were going to remain extremely vigilant. With his newly acquired shares of Citicorp, Alwaleed had also bought himself a very high profile in the United States. His moves would be scrutinized by regulators and investors alike. The rumors that Alwaleed was investing money on behalf of Middle Eastern investors that don't want their identities revealed continued to dog him. The accusations were adamantly denied by Alwaleed—and are still denied to this day. (Those who know him say the Prince sees himself as a link between the Arab world and America—a Saudi with a soft spot for true capitalism.)

A Source Emerges

Then, in the Spring of 1991 shortly after the Citicorp investment, the Bank of Credit and Commerce International (BCCI) scandal ripped through the banking world like a missile. The fifth largest private bank in the world, as it turned out, was nothing but a fraud-ridden front, laundering money for drug lords and terrorists throughout the Middle East. BCCI was also trying to gain control of American banks. It was a scandal of epic proportions that brought down dozens of high-profile members of the international banking community. It was the largest bank fraud case ever. And it didn't bode well for the Citicorp deal.

After BCCI, the media speculated that Alwaleed might be up to the same thing. In an interview with CNBC 10 years later, Alwaleed described the situation like this, "We had Arabs involved with BCCI at that time. And they had a big scandal there, unfortunately. They (the Fed) looked at what I had there, we had a big discussion, long discussions, they could not find anything wrong with it at all. But I got the message that they were in a difficult position."

The Fed was indeed in a difficult position in trying to save Citicorp—the nation's largest bank. According to one person involved in the Citicorp negotiations, the Fed suspected that the money Alwaleed was investing was not his own, and officials there "looked the other way." The source says that the lack of due diligence in adhering to the rules that require transparency of foreign investors facilitated the Fed's goal of saving Citicorp. A source close to Alwaleed now says that at least some of the money belonged to Prince Sultan bin Abdulaziz, Saudi Arabia's defense minister. The defense minister could not be reached for comment, and the Prince maintains that all of the money he invested was his. Since the Citicorp flap, Alwaleed has regularly, and voluntarily, disclosed selected investments to the public, even though he is under no obligation to do so. But he only discloses what he wants to.

Despite its controversial nature, the Citicorp deal put both Carlyle and Alwaleed on the map. Many believed the deal was the financial embodiment of the political accord between the United States and Saudi Arabia. In a *Washington Post* article at the time of the deal, Shafiqul Islam, senior fellow at the Council on Foreign Relations in New York, said "here the profit motive and the political motive seem to coincide. Right now, the Saudis are our good friends, and Citicorp does need the money." Politically, it could be considered as a quid pro quo for the United States "helping them" in the Gulf War. It was a rare time when the United States and Saudi Arabia were both politically and financially aligned, and it opened a brief window of opportunity for Carlyle and the Prince. But it wouldn't always be that way.

Surprisingly, considering the magnitude of the deal, Norris and Carlyle walked away with a mere $50,000 of the Prince's money (they were paid more handsomely by Citicorp, though they won't disclose how much). And the Prince? After a nervous year during which the Prince's investments were underwater—a time when Rubenstein routinely fretted over Citicorp's languishing stock—today's estimates fall somewhere between an $8 billion and $12 billion profit on the deal. It made all the trouble seem worth it. And it set Carlyle up for a future with the Prince, including another major bailout by Alwaleed of Euro Disney (an investment that hasn't turned out so well). But more importantly, the deal gave Carlyle access to Saudi Arabia, a country of unimaginable wealth if one knew where to look. "The deal gave us an enormously high profile in Saudi Arabia," recalls Norris. And with the Prince on its side, Carlyle had the world's best tour guide to pry open the treasures of Saudi Arabia.

7

VINNELL'S EXECUTIVE MERCENARIES

We train people to pull triggers.
> —A potential Vinnell employee, *Newsweek,*
> February 24, 1975

Cast of Characters

Henry Jackson   Former U.S. senator.

Richard Secord   Retired Air Force general, ex-employee of Vinnell,
Iran-Contra fall guy.

After its early buyout misadventures, Carlyle had finally tasted fortune in both the BDM deal and its work with the Prince. In 1992, the time came to combine their newfound successes, when BDM, by then already under Carlyle's ownership, bought a little known company of ambiguous ownership named Vinnell. The deal would marry Carlyle's burgeoning expertise in defense with its incipient relationships in the Middle East. And it would forever strengthen the political ties between two of the world's most powerful countries.

Vinnell is the clearest example of Carlyle's business inside the Iron Triangle. It combines all of the necessary elements of the military, government, and big business, in one neat, utterly secretive package. Vinnell defines the term *war profiteer,* a private company that trains foreign militaries in times of need, and would ultimately make Carlyle an insidious force inside the Kingdom of Saudi Arabia. Vinnell is yet another company with a highly controversial past that Carlyle snapped up, only to heighten its questionable legacy. Vinnell's history, before, during, and after Carlyle owned it, is a litany of covert operations, mercenary missions, and cover-ups: right up Carlyle's alley. Carlyle, it seemed, was building an entire portfolio of controversy, and Vinnell was the early centerpiece.

The relationship between the United States and Saudi Arabia has grown increasingly complex and co-dependent in recent years: the United States gorging itself on Saudi Arabia's cheap oil, and the Saudi's relying on American military support of the royal family. This give-and-take relationship has made navigating the post-September 11 political waters very tricky. Despite a near total lack of cooperation in the bombing campaign of Afghanistan and the investigation into September 11, Saudi Arabia remains the United States' chief ally in the Gulf. In response to Saudi Arabia's obstruction, senators have come out with strong rhetoric toward the Saudis, calling the regime corrupt. Some have accused them of sponsoring terror, or at least doing nothing to abate it. Others have recommended an end to the alliance between the two nations. But the relationship, however tenuous, holds. Like the oil that trades hands between the two countries, the United States holds Saudi Arabia in a slippery, combustible embrace.

Saudi Arabia's military dependence on the United States can be traced back to a Vinnell deal in 1975 that would alter the nature of the alliance forever. Of all the military ties the United States has fostered with Saudi Arabia over the last three decades, perhaps no one company has done as much to inject the American military machine into everyday life in Saudi Arabia than Vinnell. It was, and still is, an integral part of the Saudi military makeup.

A Company with No Past

Until Carlyle, through BDM, purchased Vinnell in 1992, the company virtually didn't exist to the public. Even though Vinnell claims to have been around since the days of the Great Depression, documentation of its history is nearly impossible to find. No publicity, no press releases, no news clippings. To this day, no one knows who the original owners were. Reports indicate that Vinnell, at one time a heavy construction company in Los Angeles, built Dodger Stadium. Then the company built some airstrips in Vietnam. But it wasn't until 1975 that the company mistakenly flew temporarily above the radar and into the public's view.

In February 1975, the Associated Press broke a story that sent shock waves through Washington. A private American firm was hired by the Pentagon to train Saudi troops to protect oil fields from potential aggression in the Middle East. The news came just two years after the United States had pulled its final remaining troops out of Vietnam, and Americans saw the action as yet another ill-conceived involvement in a foreign nation's affairs. Only this time, it wasn't enlisted soldiers, working for the American Armed Forces. It was soldiers of fortune, civilians with guns.

The $77 million contract, brokered through the Defense Department, stipulated that Vinnell would hire 1,000 former Special Forces personnel, most of whom had recently served in Vietnam, to work with the Saudi National Guard, the 26,000 men sworn to protect the royal family. Never before had a private company, employing civilians, been deployed overseas to train a foreign government in battle tactics. But it would not be the last time.

The news caused instant outrage on Capitol Hill. Congressmen accused the Pentagon of hiring "mercenaries" to develop the military of a country the United States may one day have to invade. At the time, U.S. oil companies complained incessantly to congressmen that Saudi Arabia and the Middle East were strangling the United States by manipulating the exportation of oil. Henry Kissinger himself had threatened an invasion of Saudi Arabia if the situation did not improve. With tensions rising between the two nations, the Vinnell deal left lawmakers scratching their heads. Senator Henry Jackson, of Washington, demanded a congressional inquiry and was quoted as saying he was "completely baffled," by the deal, adding that to his knowledge, the only threat to Saudi Arabia's oil fields had come from the United States itself. And we certainly weren't going to train the Saudi National Guard how to defend themselves against us, were we?

U.S. companies had regularly scored contracts for training foreign nations in the use of American-made military equipment. But training men in battlefield tactics and combat was considered off limits. It was viewed by many as a way for the government to get around laws that prohibit the United States from getting involved militarily in certain nations, an issue that was particularly raw following America's disastrous foray into Vietnam. It was a quiet, though expensive, way to further America's agenda abroad without committing its own troops.

The type of men Vinnell was recruiting for the job led to consternation from others in the military training industry. This was not your typical service contract. The head of one security company at the time of the deal told *Forbes* that "the whole thing stinks. You're talking about professional killers, very senior Special Forces guys on this Vinnell contract. These aren't personnel specialists. They've got tremendous combat reputations. What kind of control does Vinnell have over them once they get over there?"

In the same article, William L. Hilger, corporate secretary for Vinnell at the time of the deal, told *Forbes,* "This isn't anything new for us. We've done all this sort of stuff with the Chinese Nationalists, the South Koreans, the South Vietnamese . . . We teach them to rebuild their ordnance equipment, repair their vehicles for them, operate and maintain their airbases, their drydocks, install and operate their power system, everything."

The Pentagon, embarrassed by the press leak of the deal, went into defense mode, assuring Americans that the Vinnell personnel would not be instructing the Saudi National Guard in ground tactics and maneuvers (Vinnell employees were seen fighting with Saudi troops in the Gulf War 15 years later). Defense Department spokesmen explained that the United States was trying to wean foreign governments off of U.S. military manpower, steering them toward private companies instead, which frees up active troops for more pressing action. It was the beginning of privatization in the defense industry, a trend that would burgeon over the following two decades and make Carlyle very rich. The Vinnell contract was characterized as a one-time training mission, a quick in-and-out. Twenty-seven years later, Vinnell is still well entrenched in Saudi Arabia, though Carlyle sold the company in 1997.

At the time, Vinnell spokespeople played down the significance of the announcement, defending themselves against claims that they were nothing but a ragtag group of mercenaries. One former U.S. Army officer, while waiting in line to apply for a position in Saudi Arabia (Vinnell had to hire on most of the men for the job due to a lack of experience in this type of work), told *Newsweek* "We're not mercenaries because we're not pulling the triggers. We train people to pull triggers." Hundreds of young men applied for the positions, which were advertised in local newspapers. It was a truly frightening trend for Americans to watch evolve.

Senator Henry Jackson finally got his congressional investigation into the Vinnell deal. And the results were difficult to fathom. The probe yielded a stunning contract clause that barred Jews from working on the contract. Because of the sensitivities between Arabs and Jews, which ran very high in the mid-1970s, Vinnell had agreed to the obviously anti-Semitic clause. The investigation also turned up a suspicious $4.5 million agent's fee that investigators thought was a kickback to the royal family. But in the end, the anti-Semitic clause was dropped, and no charges were filed. Vinnell was free to go ahead with the highly controversial, highly profitable, contract in Saudi Arabia.

Going Dark

Then Vinnell disappeared again. Like a shadow at night, the company seemed to have the disconcerting ability to disappear when it needed to, just go dark. It wasn't until the Iran-Contra affair that Vinnell resurfaced temporarily. Richard Secord, a retired Air Force general who worked for Vinnell in the mid-1980s, was implicated as Oliver North's accomplice in the well-known arms-for-hostages scandal. As part of the voluminous press coverage of the scandal, Secord's background was thoroughly investigated, and it was found that he had previously worked for Vinnell. But Vinnell managed to successfully distance itself from the investigation and from Secord, who would eventually plead guilty to lying to Congress for his involvement with Iran-Contra. But his involvement with Vinnell put the quiet company in the spotlight once again.

In a brief, confusing, and rare public reference to the company, a *Time* magazine article in 1987 picked up the scent of Vinnell when it reported that two Vinnell employees may have been tangentially involved in a failed attempt to overthrow Granada's leftist Prime Minister Maurice Bishop. It was a bizarre revelation and few in the media knew what to make of it. What were these guys doing? And does this mean Vinnell was involved with plots of regime change? The story caused a few ripples of concern, no follow-up, and then once again the company dropped off the radar. How was such an intriguing company keeping so quiet? Why did the press never seem to follow up on these strange tales?

By the time Carlyle picked up Vinnell, via BDM, in March 1992, the company had built the Saudi National Guard up to about 70,000 troops from the original 26,000. It had also paved the way for the cooperation between the United States and Saudi Arabia in the Gulf War. Many of its employees fought right alongside the Saudis, something the Pentagon had promised would never happen, in defending Saudi Arabia from Iraq's aggression. "During the Gulf War, when a lot of companies sent their people home, BDM (and Vinnell) did not," says Phil Odeen, then chairman of BDM. "We kept our people there during war, and we got high marks from the Saudi's for that. I'm sure there were a lot of nervous people, but that was a big factor in our continued success in Saudi Arabia."

The U.S. military presence in Saudi Arabia was growing steadily after the war. The Air Force was setting up shop indefinitely in Riyadh. BDM was increasing its business. By the mid-1990s, there were about 5,000 U.S. military personnel in Saudi Arabia, and close to 2,000 BDM and Vinnell employees. But while the royal family welcomed the presence of the American military machine in its backyard, many Saudi nationals did not. It is a dichotomy that exists to this day, in which the royal family's concerns do not mirror those of the general population of Saudi Arabia. And Vinnell's presence in Saudi Arabia was exacerbating that problem. Both the royal family and Vinnell tried to keep their dealings as quiet as possible. But with so many non-Arab employees working in and around Riyadh, the secret got out. Tensions steadily rose, and then, disaster struck.

Hate Boils Over

In November 1995, a car bomb ripped through the Riyadh offices of BDM and Vinnell, killing seven people, including five Americans. Three spouses of Vinnell employees were injured in the blast. The offices that were targeted were those supporting Vinnell's National Guard contract. "One of them got cut up badly," remembers Odeen. Unlike a U.S. embassy, a typical target for this kind of terrorism, the building that housed Vinnell's people were purposely nondescript. The workers kept as low a profile as possible. Vinnell's employees knew they were an unwelcome presence to the majority of the population. "There was a fair amount of security concern," recalls Odeen. "You didn't drive around with an American flag in your car." But it didn't matter. The radicals responsible for the explosion knew enough to attack the Americans where they worked. Vinnell was fooling nobody.

The bombing set off a feeding frenzy by the national media. It was as though the Vinnell story was brand new, and everyone had questions. What were these people doing in Saudi Arabia? How did the Saudis know they were there? Why were they targets? The answers would turn out to be far more sinister than anyone suspected.

According to one former board member of Vinnell, who wishes to remain anonymous, Vinnell had been a cover for the CIA for decades. Dating all the way back to 1975, the company was gathering intelligence on behalf of the U.S. government, by infiltrating the Saudi National Guard under the specious guise of military trainers. The board member also says that though the company was supposed to be nothing more than a front for covert intelligence gathering, the darn thing started making money. The board member likened the operation to the Hollywood movie *Swordfish* starring John Travolta, in which secret operatives from the government end up making a fortune off of companies designed to be fronts for the Drug Enforcement Agency.

According to this board member, even after BDM purchased Vinnell in 1992, there was very little anyone on the board did in terms of overseeing of Vinnell. Board members met regularly, but rarely was anything acted upon. The company that seemed to run itself was, in fact, being run by someone else.

If true, the company's murky history starts to make more sense. The ambiguous ownership. The fits of secrecy. The peripheral involvement in Iran-Contra and Granada. And finally, the targeting of Vinnell by Saudi nationals. For his part, Odeen demurs when presented with this revelation. "I know nothing about it being a CIA front," says Odeen. "I knew it to be a first-rate training organization." But first-hand sources, one of whom sat side by side with Odeen on the Vinnell board, say otherwise.

Today, Vinnell continues to do its work in Saudi Arabia, since 1997 as a subsidiary of TRW. Whether it is a front for CIA activity is unclear. The company is among many that have come under political attack in the wake of September 11, and has been held up as an example of why it is so difficult for the United States to cut ties with the Saudis during the War on Terrorism. William Hartung, a foreign policy expert at the World Policy Institute, in referring to Saudi Arabia's stonewalling of the United States following September 11, was quoted as saying "If there weren't all these other arrangements—arms deals and oil deals and consultancies—I don't think the United States would stand for this lack of cooperation." And it's not just Vinnell. The company led a tidal wave of private American military into Saudi Arabia. Today, it is estimated that between 35,000 and 45,000 employees for outfits like Vinnell are living and working in Saudi Arabia. It is becoming nearly impossible to distinguish America's real military from America's soldiers for hire.

Carlyle has certainly had more pedestrian investments than Vinnell, but it's had more controversial ones as well. It's safe to say, that after the purchase of Vinnell, Carlyle entered new territory that separated the company from other buyout giants like Kohlberg Kravis Roberts and Co. Alleged CIA cover ups, car bombs, purported executive mercenaries may sound like a Hollywood movie script or a far-fetched work of fiction, but it's all in a day's work for Carlyle.

8

OUT OF THE SHADOWS

A Republican administration in exile.
> —*Time* magazine, March 22, 1993

Cast of Characters

James Baker III	Carlyle executive, former secretary of state under President George Bush Sr.
Richard Darman	Carlyle executive, former director of the Office of Management and Budget under President George Bush Sr.
Colin Powell	Former Carlyle advisor, secretary of state under President George W. Bush.
Michael Eisner	Chairman of Walt Disney.
Antonio Guizzetti	Italian business man, friend of Steve Norris.
Basil Al Rahim	Former Carlyle employee in charge of raising capital in Middle East.
Stephen Norris	
William Conway	

By the beginning of 1993, Carlyle was a somewhat seasoned, if not terribly successful, private equity firm. Six years and a dozen or so buyouts after Rubenstein and Norris joined forces at the Carlyle Hotel in New York, the firm had made some huge deals happen. It had also participated in some major flops. The company had stakes in 10 companies valued at around $2 billion.

But the bottom line was that the Carlyle was not making the gobs of money its co-founders had hoped it would. And the time had come to kick it into gear.

In 1993, Carlyle began a rapid transformation, from an eager young private equity firm into an international political and financial powerhouse. They brought in the high-priced, high-profile talent that would ultimately define the company. They shed some of their old, bad habits, one of which happened to be Steve Norris, the co-founder of the company. And the result was nothing short of astounding. The moves the company made between 1993 and 1995 would cause some growing pains within the firm, but would also lay the groundwork for the new Carlyle—the company kicked off the training wheels and began to tear around the international business community. All of which began with a very important hire, and ended with a tragic but inevitable firing.

To this point, the company was still operating without a chairman. Carlucci had settled nicely into his role as vice chairman. Aside from opening the doors of defense to the Carlyle Group, he was now residing on the boards of an astounding 32 companies, not all of them owned by Carlyle. He was ridiculously well connected. His time was precious, and he was not highly involved in Carlyle's day-to-day deal making. While Carlucci was a serviceable figurehead, he was a bit detached, and didn't exactly reek of credibility. In referring to Carlucci's status value and lack of business acumen, Rubenstein was often overheard around the office saying, "we all know what Frank is . . ." Carlucci was invaluable in Carlyle's dealings in defense. But he was not the marquee name the company needed to really go global. Carlyle needed someone who could help raise money. Someone that would make the world stand up and take notice. Someone universally admired and respected. Someone like James A. Baker III.

A Trophy Hire

Baker, like Carlucci and Rumsfeld, attended Princeton University, and graduated in 1952. (The more you research the backgrounds of the key figures in Carlyle, the more you end up at the same place: Princeton.) He then spent almost 20 years toiling with Houston law firm, Andrews and Kurth. But in 1975, he would enter American politics when he became the Undersecretary of Commerce for then President Ford. He would not leave politics again for the next 18 years. During that time, he would lead presidential campaigns for Ford, Reagan, and Bush. He would serve as Reagan's White House Chief of Staff from 1981 to 1985, then secretary of the Treasury from 1985 to 1988. After leading George H. W. Bush to victory in the 1988 presidential election, he would be rewarded by becoming the nation's sixty-first secretary of state, a post he would hold from January 1989 to August 1992. For the last few months of Bush's time in office, Baker again became White House chief of staff, until January 1993, when after failing to get his boss reelected, he resignedly cleaned out his office to make way for the incoming President Clinton, ushering in eight long years of Democrats in the White House.

All told, Baker had been camped in the White House for 12 years straight. He was, and still is, a consummate statesman, and a steadfast Republican. Carlyle, with its offices at 1001 Pennsylvania Avenue, just a few blocks from the White House, with a distinctly Republican flavor, made a compelling offer to Baker. It's not as if Baker had a paucity of offers either. Publishers urged him to write his memoirs. Rice University, in Baker's hometown of Houston, wanted him to run a foundation. Enron made overtures. So when the boys from Carlyle knocked on his door, they weren't sure what to expect.

Rubenstein, Conway, and Norris went to the White House to make their pitch during the White House transition, and in the waiting room, they ran into David Rockefeller, the next in line to see the man of the hour. They knew then that the competition for Baker's services was going to be stiff. After an hour-long meeting with Baker, however, they felt considerably better about their chances of landing the outgoing administration's biggest fish (aside from the president himself, of course). Baker was intrigued by the offer, and he invited Richard Darman, Bush's outgoing budget director, to get involved. Darman convinced Rubenstein that if Carlyle wanted Baker, they were going to have to take him, too. He made it a package deal.

On February 24, 1993, the news release hit the wire that Richard Darman, former director of the Office of Management and Budget, was joining the Carlyle Group as a managing director. Darman was a former executive at Shearson Lehman Hutton, Inc., and combined with his years of government service, would make an excellent investment advisor in sectors heavily affected by government regulation, like energy, transportation, and insurance. Two weeks later, days after accepting another job consulting with Enron on overseas projects, James Baker became a partner at the Carlyle Group. Carlyle had officially appeared on the radar screen.

Suddenly, every media outlet wanted to find out more about this quiet little merchant bank called the Carlyle Group, and it seemed that every writer had the same idea. Ten days after Baker was hired, *Time* magazine ran a story entitled "Peddling Power for Profit." In it, the magazine referred to Carlyle as a "Republican administration in exile," and reported that Colin Powell was also considering a job offer from the group. Powell and Carlucci were very close from their days together on Reagan's National Security Council. Then the *New Republic* wrote a scathing cover story later that year entitled "The Access Capitalists," which portrayed Rubenstein as a nervous, paranoid wreck, obsessed with the media's portrayal of Carlyle. His fears proved warranted. In a *New Republic* article, writer Michael Lewis called the company a "salon des refuses for the influence peddling class." It went on to say, "[Carlyle] offers a neat solution for people who don't have a lot to sell besides their access, but who don't want to appear to be selling their access." It was not the kind of public relations coup Rubenstein was looking for when he went combing through the remains of the former Republican White House. The stinging accusations and acrid characterizations first levied in these articles would follow the company to this day.

Baker's hiring caused some waves inside Carlyle as well. Rubenstein and Norris, who were running the firm at this point, were concerned that Carlucci would want out when Baker came on board. After all, it would be hard to argue that Carlucci would be of more value to the company than Baker. It seemed reasonable to assume that Baker might be Carlucci's boss. It wasn't clear which one was going to be more senior. So in a preemptive case of ego-stroking, the firm decided to bring Baker in as a partner and promote Carlucci to chairman. But former employees agree that the new title was purely for outside appearances. One former employee would say of Carlucci, "Frank was a good guy to have around, even though he was rarely there. But when we had a tough problem to tackle, no one said, 'Hey, let's go show this to Frank and see what he comes up with.'" Carlucci and Baker also clashed over politics. When he was in the Carlyle offices, Carlucci was often overheard badmouthing former President Reagan, the man who appointed him national security advisor and secretary of defense, saving him from the nightmare that was Sears World Trade. Baker, a devoted Reaganite, didn't take lightly to Carlucci's disrespect. And Norris, a huge Reagan fan, would often remind Carlucci that it was Reagan who "made you who you are," a jab that went unappreciated by Carlucci. But Carlucci and Baker's differences were miniscule compared to the other clashes to come in Carlyle's testosterone-laden executive ranks.

Darman and Rubenstein's personalities clashed badly early on. Rubenstein phoned Norris in Paris one day to say he had reached the end of his rope and that something had to be done. It was a classic style clash. The two eventually had to work out an arrangement limiting Darman's role in management in order to get along. The tensions inside the company were growing along with the company itself. As with any company that achieves success, Carlyle was finding itself at a crossroad between the past and the future, and the strain was weighing on its executives. Power struggles were common, and not the least bit private. The entire office saw management openly sniping at one another. But no one could have understood the severity of the split that had opened up between fellow co-founders Steve Norris and Bill Conway. And this was the battle that would be the turning point in Carlyle's history, the winner defining how business would be done going forward, the loser left to carve out another future, away from Carlyle.

A Chasm of Character

Norris' relationship with Conway had almost completely deteriorated by the mid-1990s. There were major differences of opinion on business issues. But this particular feud got increasingly personal over the years. Two men could not have had more wildly disparate styles. Norris loved "elephant hunting," wheeling and dealing, striking out occasionally, but all the while looking for the deal of the century, the one that would make them all rich beyond their dreams. He spent money lavishly, spoke out of turn, and followed his own instincts. Some call him mercurial, a term he dismisses by claiming not to know the definition. Some call him a loose cannon. But no one denies the important impact that Norris had on Carlyle. "In the beginning, it was all Steve," recalls one employee. "David and Steve. Steve and David. That was all anybody knew. Between the two of them, they got it all done."

Conway, on the other hand, was conservative to a fault. He deplored wastefulness and railed against unnecessary expenses. He was a button-down businessman from New England. His father wrote the book on quality . . . literally. William E. Conway Sr., a world-renowned quality consultant, first wrote *The Quality Secret: The Right Way to Manage* in 1996, and followed it up with *Winning the War on Waste: Changing the Way We Work* in 1997. Conway's father was also the first American CEO to embrace the teachings of Total Quality Management (TQM), a corporate trend that would sweep through American business as capriciously as the Macarena affected American dance. Knowing this, it is not difficult to understand why Conway found Norris' footloose style of deal making deeply offensive. And why Norris felt threatened by Conway's staid approach to business. If you didn't know any better, you'd have thought Conway was playing the role of controlling father to Norris' troubled adolescent in Carlyle's internal drama.

The rift between the two was damaging morale at the Carlyle offices. Without solidarity at the top, there was little to keep the younger MBA types from fracturing and feeling put upon. One former employee remembers the office at the time like this: "It was not a place where you sensed joy or even teamwork. There was no camaraderie. It was a tough place to be, where most of the economics went to the senior guys, and they didn't even like each other. It was hard for the younger guys to see how they were ever going to make money. A huge amount of the firm was going to a bunch of guys who didn't even do deals." Things got even worse, and even pettier.

Norris recalls a painting he bought for about $5,000 for his wife at the time that hung in his living room. Later when the Norrises hosted a cocktail party at their home, Conway and his wife saw the painting and were beside themselves. Apparently, Conway's wife had intended to buy the same painting. According to Norris, the rivalry between the two had grown so fierce, that the

Conways were convinced that Norris had bought the painting just to stick it to them. Norris claims he had no idea the Conways had designs on the painting. The petty jealousies and name calling of the super rich can be astonishing to the rest of us.

By 1993, it had become appallingly clear that Norris' time with the firm was going to end badly. Conway had begun to manage Carlyle's defense buyout business, taking over the day-to-day deal-making responsibilities that Carlucci had helped put in place. By this time, Norris was spending a great deal of time and money setting up shop in Paris as he worked a deal between the Prince Al-waleed and Euro Disney, an operation badly in need of some financing. Norris wasn't afraid to enjoy his successes, and when he was in Paris on business, he stayed at the Ritz Carlton. He also availed himself of some free time while traveling on business. He didn't dwell on the minutia of high finance. He likes to tell a story that illustrates the difference in work ethics between himself and David Rubenstein. Bill Conway came in to the Carlyle offices one weekend to pick up some work. Rubenstein was there, huddled over his desk, feverishly writing a memo, with Norris relaxing on his couch. Conway asked Rubenstein what he was doing, and David said, "writing a memo." Norris and Conway teased him, until Rubenstein asked Conway what he liked to do to relax, to which Conway replied, "play golf." Rubenstein then said, "Think of this as me playing golf." Suffice to say given Norris' position on the couch, he didn't write memos to relax.

While Norris was negotiating with Michael Eisner and crew for the Prince's eventual $360 million investment into Euro Disney, he was racking up healthy expense reports. One day, in the midst of heated negotiations, he decided to go shopping. "I could see that it wasn't going anywhere," Norris says of the negotiations. "If I wasn't available, nobody could talk to anybody, and tempers would calm down, and we could reach a compromise." It was a decision for which Conway could never forgive him. Carlyle eventually did get the deal done, but the folks back in Washington objected to the amount of money it was costing them and Norris' laissez-faire attitude in Paris. Norris claims that he could have spent less money, but not much less. However, in talking about this contentious time in the company's history, he lets slip, "I was in my suite at the Ritz . . . well, my room at the Ritz . . . I was accused of having a suite, but I really didn't."

By this time, Norris alienated the Prince by turning down a job offer from him, pissed off Michael Eisner during the Disney negotiations, and ran up a monster expense tab in Paris. His partners were losing patience. "He has no discipline," says Stan Anderson, a partner at McDermott Will & Emery in Washington, who worked with Carlyle, especially Baker, on a few early deals. "On a bike trip in Europe, Eisner lambasted him for bringing an undisciplined approach to the negotiations," says Anderson. "He was basically living in Paris, and he was living too large."

Norris' Last Stand

The final straw for Norris came when he drummed up a potential piece of business with a man he met in a sauna. (Norris and saunas seem to have a long history at Carlyle—rumors abound at Carlyle about Norris' alleged sexual exploits with a female employee in the Carlyle office's sauna, an adventure that allegedly ended badly when it triggered the fire alarm and evacuated the building—a rumor that Norris flatly denies but other former employees swear is true.) After a workout, Norris started up a conversation with an Italian businessman in the steam room of their fitness club. The man was Antonio Guizzetti, the Washington, DC, representative of ENI, a massive Italian oil exploration firm. Norris smelled a deal. "He wanted to internationalize Carlyle," recalls Guizzetti. "To that point, Carlyle International didn't exist."

Norris and Guizzetti struck up a friendship. It was classic Norris, always looking for deals, even in the sauna. The two tried all sorts of deals at first. They met with Italian designer Giorgio Armani. They met with Paolo Bulgari, of Bulgari Jewelers and nearly cinched a deal to buy 10 percent of the company for only $5 million. ("If we had finalized the deal with the Bulgaris we would be multimillionaires right now," laments Guizzetti.) But in the end, the deal they decided to pursue was a buyout of IP, the retail unit of Italian oil company AGIP, a subsidiary of ENI. AGIP had built up too large a market share in Italy with IP, and the European Union was uncomfortable with the potential for monopoly, so the company was looking to sell off the retail chain of gas stations. Because the deal would have major political implications within Italy and the United States, Carlyle assigned a career diplomat to assist Norris. They called in Baker.

Guizzetti, Norris, and Baker traveled around Italy meeting with ENI's top executives as well as high-ranking politicians. They secured time with then Prime Minister Carlo Azeglio Ciampi's general secretary. The met multiple times with Paolo Savona, the minister of industry privatization. Guizzetti said traveling with Baker was like traveling with royalty. "We flew in a private jet and had meetings with everybody," gushes Guizzetti. "Traveling with James Baker in Italy guaranteed that the deal was serious."

The deal was serious, and Norris began rounding up financing. Through a new Carlyle colleague named Basil Al Rahim, who had been traveling throughout the Middle East to raise money, Carlyle was put in touch with an extremely wealthy family in Saudi Arabia that wanted in on the deal. The family had amassed a fortune through construction contracts and was looking to diversify. The name of the family was bin Laden. And the relationship Al Rahim established with the estranged family of Osama bin Laden would go on to be a long-term and very lucrative partnership. But not this time.

With financing in place, regulatory issues cleared with the help of Baker, and AGIP ready to sell, Norris was suddenly asked to leave Carlyle in January 1995. The public face on the resignation was that Norris no longer wanted to be bothered with managing money, when his real passion was for cutting deals. Rubenstein was quoted in the *Washington Post* saying "Steve is one of the most creative deal-doers in the country. He wants to do different types of deals from what we want to do." According to Norris, the reality was far more contentious and personal. Conway's cautious conservativism had won out, and Norris was to be part of Carlyle's past, not its future.

Without Norris, the IP deal fell apart. Carlyle backed out of the transaction at the eleventh hour, claiming that one of AGIP's oil refineries processed oil from Libya, a nation embargoed by the United States for sponsoring terrorism. Norris says that Baker's law firm, Baker Botts, had already told Carlyle there were no legal problems with owning the refinery. But Carlyle wanted out anyway, apparently preferring to distance itself from deals that were initiated by Norris. "We were very, very close to the deal," recalls Guizzetti. "Then suddenly Carlyle changed, and the reason they gave about Libya being a terrorist state was stupid. It was the departure of Steve [Norris] that killed the deal."

Norris went on to start up a series of independent investment houses on his own and met with tepid success. Many people in the private equity world say that Carlyle made it very difficult for Norris to succeed after he left. "They badmouthed him all over Europe," says one banker. "It made it impossible for him to raise money." A number of bizarre rumors had begun to crop up around the Beltway, like the one about the sauna, about Norris' relationships and spending habits. To this day, Norris is baffled by the animosity he curried while at Carlyle, and questions his actions often. "I've certainly made my share of mistakes while I was there, but if I had to do it over again, I don't think I would have changed anything," he says. He blames Carlyle, particularly Conway, for waging what he terms a "scorched earth" campaign against him after he left, sullying his name and attacking his character. What is undeniable is that Norris has been completely written out of the firm's history. Deals that he said he did are now attributed to Rubenstein, Conway, or Carlucci. He is no longer mentioned in any of the company's literature. He is persona nongrata. It's as if he never existed. Poof.

"They had to discredit me," says Norris today, while waiting for his girlfriend at the Four Seasons in Washington, DC, the hotel chain that he'd helped the Prince invest in years earlier. "I should have been a hell of a lot smarter. But one of my biggest weaknesses is that I tend to be too trusting. I thought I had some partners around me that, though we all had different approaches, would pull together. That just didn't turn out to be the case."

With Norris out of the picture, and Baker in place, Carlyle was now looking toward its future. Baker's marquee value put the company in a position to start raising massive amounts of capital, a problem that had plagued them in the early stages. And now they would be able to take their dog-and-pony show on the road, raising international funds off the strength of Baker's name. The company now had enough heavy hitters to pry open wallets from South Korea to Saudi Arabia. While Baker was still having a little difficulty weaning himself from politics—on a fund-raising trip to Japan in 1994, Baker could not pull himself from the television set as he watched that year's election results come in—he would prove to be an invaluable addition to the firm. He would help attract money from some of the wealthiest people in the world. A trend that in turn would make Carlyle itself one of the biggest investors in the world.

9

BREAKING THE BANK

*When you make $50 million, you have a
different perspective on life.*
—David Rubenstein, *New Republic*, October 18, 1993

Cast of Characters

George Soros   Internationally respected investor and speculator,
Carlyle investor.

John Major   Former prime minister of the United Kingdom,
Carlyle partner.

David Rubenstein

Private equity firms are often judged on the amount of money they have under management. It is generally considered a measure of success, an indication of investors' trust and confidence. In this business, size matters. And though Carlyle had done some decent deals, they were not considered a major private equity player. They didn't have any funds of $1 billion or more, a basic earmark of a successful firm. In fact, their largest fund was a meager $100 million. They still struggled to raise enough capital to fund the deals they did identify, and even those were cobbled together using smoke and mirrors. They often took on too much debt when acquiring companies, and that would inevitably make exiting the investment more difficult. What they needed was more fund raising. They needed money in the bank. Enough money that they could stop worrying about money. The kind of money that only the elite firms could raise. They were about to get it. But like Carlyle's portfolio of acquired companies, its list of investors carried conflict and controversy. Soliciting money from just about anyone who had it, the company put together some powerful and unlikely bedfellows. And the little merchant bank from Washington, DC, began to grow in both stature and intrigue.

Considering Carlyle's questionable investing record by the mid-1990s, it is truly remarkable that the firm was able to attract the type of talent it had. Midway through the 1990s, the company had yet to cash in on anything but a few defense buyouts. Carlyle was getting pigeon holed as a defense company, and fast. Business press was criticizing it for being a bunch of tax-scamming crony capitalists, trading in on their time in government, and hitting up old friends for business. They had made a little money, but they certainly weren't lighting up the scoreboard. One magazine reported that Conway's wife was pestering him about seeing some profits they could take to the supermarket. Then everything started to change.

With Baker on board, Rubenstein turned his focus to raising money. Truckloads of money. Rubenstein began work on a fund that would eventually be called Carlyle Partners II, designed to focus on aerospace, defense, healthcare, telecommunications, and insurance. The idea was to parlay the newly acquired political expertise that Carlyle had gained through the hiring of Darman and Baker, and invest in industries that are heavily dependent on federal regulation. This way, Carlyle could cash in on its ex-politicos in two ways: first, to help them raise money by giving speeches at home and abroad, packing the house with high net worth individuals; and, two, to leverage their relationships with lawmakers to gain insight on the direction of policies that affect their target industries. It was a brilliant strategy that was about to make all of them very, very rich.

Soros' Millions

The goal for the fund was $500 million, a relatively modest sum in private equity circles, but five times as much as Carlyle had ever raised. Until this time, Carlyle's strategy was to first identify a deal, then round up the investors needed to make it happen. There was often a great deal of leverage involved, and the debt loads on some of the deals caused ongoing problems for Carlyle. This time would be different. After rounding up almost $150 million from some banks, pension funds, and Richard K. Mellon & Sons (an original investor in Carlyle), the company was going after an investor that could contribute both money and fame and get them over the hump. They were going after George Soros.

The Hungarian-American Soros already had the reputation of being the most prescient and successful investor in the world. His Quantum Fund was admired around the world. His investment record was unassailable. But on September 16, 1992, he cemented his place in finance history by shorting the British pound, and nearly bringing down the British banking system. That day came to be known as Black Wednesday.

Shorting is a way of betting that a stock or currency will lose value, usually over a relatively short amount of time. The investor borrows the stock or currency, then sells it, expecting to buy it back after the value decreases, thus pocketing the difference. It's a very risky investment strategy, because should the stock or currency increase in value during that time, the short investor may be forced to buy back the stock with money they may or may not have, resulting in huge losses. People who short are universally reviled in investing circles, because they want companies and currencies to fail and thus lose value. Often times, they take an active role in making that happen, circulating rumors and various untruths that will undermine the stock. It can be a rather dirty business.

In 1992, Britain was in the midst of a tough recession, and the British pound was struggling to maintain its value against other currencies. Then prime minister John Major had announced a comprehensive plan to restore confidence in the pound. Publicly, he called it his "over-riding objective." But Soros had other ideas.

Soros placed a $10 billion bet against the pound, enough to cause the value of the currency to bottom out on its own when the public saw that such an important and knowledgeable investor had lost confidence in the currency. In essence, Soros was betting against Major and his ability to prop up the sagging pound. It has been called the highest stakes poker game in history. Currency speculators were either to believe in Major's ability to save the pound or Soros' intent to eviscerate it. Soros won. On Black Wednesday, the pound crashed, crippling the British economy and embarrassing the prime minister. Soros made a profit of $950 million. He would later be known in England as the man who made a billion off the pound's collapse. Needless to say, George Soros wasn't exactly a popular bloke in the United Kingdom.

So when Soros agreed to become a limited partner in Carlyle's new fund exactly one year after Black Wednesday, he was bringing far more than just $100 million. He was bringing added credibility and a reputation for making gobs of money. George Soros didn't make bad investments, so the Carlyle Group must be for real. Soros was also jump starting a fund that would go on to be the most successful in Carlyle's history. It is unusual for a private equity firm to issue a press release announcing an investment into a fund. Usually contributions to private equity funds are decidedly low-key events, meant to be kept private. Most investors prefer it that way. But it's different when the investor is George Soros. Carlyle needed to capitalize on their newfound fortune. So an announcement went out hailing a new dawn at Carlyle. Rubenstein would publicly characterize the investment as "more of a partnership than just a passive relationship." Indeed, Soros helped to market the fund, and his anchor investment brought the total money raised to half the anticipated $500 million. But as it turned out, reaching the stated goal of $500 million would not be a problem for Carlyle, now that they could throw Soros' name around at meetings.

Suddenly, raising money was surprisingly easy. Investments were pouring in from the likes of American Airlines, Gannett, Citibank, and others. By the winter of 1994, the fund had already reached $400 million, and the target was raised to $650 million. Then in the fall of 1995, the goal was again raised, this time to $750 million. The money was starting to pile up. The Carlyle Group had everyone from Soros to Colin Powell helping them out, talking to investors, and opening wallets.

In Carlyle's previous fund, Carlyle Partners I, the defense investments Carlyle had made in the late 1980s were finally starting to cash out in the mid-1990s, and the payment was handsome. The company took a $38 million investment in Vought Aircraft in 1992, turned the company around, then sold it to Northrop Grumman just two years later for $130 million. Word got around quickly that Carlyle had the best game in town. Rumors of 46 percent annual rates of return had investors salivating. Members of the bin Laden family were in for untold millions. The state of Florida was in for $200 million. And the California Public Employees' Retirement System (CalPERS) was in for $80 million.

By the time Carlyle Partners II closed in September 1996, the fund had raised more than $1.3 billion, 13 times the size of the company's first fund, and more than twice the anticipated amount. The billion dollar mark is an important right of passage for any private equity firm, and Carlyle had now reached the levels of the elite. From this massive fund, the company would spread its investments all over the defense world. Carlyle Partners II was, and still is, the company's crown jewel. Many more funds would come down the line, but none with the power, scope, and success of Carlyle Partners II.

The Rich Get Richer

The time had come to start investing the money the company had worked so hard to raise. And true to its word, Carlyle sunk the bulk of the cash into an impressive series of defense, aerospace, and security companies. Names like Aerostructures Corp., United Defense, United States Marine Repair, and U.S. Investigations Services dominated the list of investments. And most of them had one thing in common: They depended on government contracts to make a living. Carlyle Partners II would ultimately go on to become the source of massive controversy, but before that it would make a killing, returning better than 30 percent annually to its investors, and finally making Carlyle's co-founders very, very rich.

Carlyle was really starting to hit its stride in the mid-1990s, both in raising capital and cutting deals. No deal illustrates that better than Howmet, a maker of blades that go into jet engines and gas turbines. In the fall of 1995, a major French multinational corporation called Pechiney was looking to unload Howmet quickly and quietly. Part of Carlyle's strategy in identifying investments—the company was looking at more than 1,200 potential deals a year at this point, but rarely invested in more than four or five—was to avoid getting into an auction with all of the other big names in private equity, like Kohlberg Kravis & Roberts or Forstmann Little & Co. As it turned out, the big guys weren't interested anyway, because the aerospace industry was in a major slump. So Carlyle joined forces with a maker of rocket fuel named Thiokol, and each picked up half of Howmet for $100 million. The two companies leveraged the rest of the purchase, which ended up costing $750 million in total. They all agreed they had overpaid.

Carlyle then applied a formula that would result in many successes for them in the future. They structured a sweeping system of financial incentives, from the executives to the shop floor workers. Stock options for upper management, and straight bonuses for the grunts. They taught every last employee in the company, all 10,000 of them, how to manage cash flow. They dangled a great big green carrot. And it worked. In the first two years Carlyle owned the company, sales increased by 25 percent while expenses fell consistently.

By the fall of 1997, just two years after the buyout, Carlyle had managed to pay down more than half the debt that was incurred during the buyout and was ready to take Howmet public. The initial public offering was valued at $1.5 billion. Carlyle was entitled to half of that, making their $100 million investment worth $750 million. Not bad for a two-year turnaround. The boys at Carlyle had learned much since the early days of Chi-Chi's and Caterair. Things were starting to come more easily for them.

Carlyle was on a serious roll now. They decided to hit the global scene, using the same formula they had applied domestically: hire ex-politicos to open doors and wallets. By this time the company had George Bush Sr. casually working for them on and off as a "senior advisor." (Bush and Rubenstein had become very close friends at this point.) So it wasn't difficult to hook former U.K. Prime Minister John Major, as well. Fresh off his 16 years in government, the last seven of which were as prime minister, Major was another huge score for Carlyle. He had been America's ally during the Gulf War, which put him largely in the good graces of Carlyle's Middle East investors. And Carlyle had plans to create another massive buyout fund, this time targeted at European companies. The fit was perfect, and in late 1997, John Major became a member of the Carlyle European Advisory Board—just months after he left his post as prime minister in May.

The hiring of Major set up another of Carlyle's global ironies. It was, of course, Major that fought so hard to restore the value of the pound during Britain's disastrous recession in the early 1990s. And it was Soros who had opposed him; almost single-handedly defeating Major's efforts by speculating on the pound, and bringing the British economy to its knees. Now they were partners in their business with Carlyle. Apparently, world leaders can forgive and forget. Nothing personal. With all that behind them, it was time to party.

The company held a lavish celebration marking its tenth anniversary in the fall of 1997. Inside the Library of Congress, the capitol building visible through the windows, the Carlyle Group celebrated its success with a gala affair that included a 20-piece orchestra. The room was wall-to-wall dignitaries, world leaders, ex-presidents, and business leaders. The Carlyle gala was the place to be, the tough ticket in DC. These were good times, and the partners at Carlyle knew it. They had finally made it.

Globalization

The European fund, like Carlyle Partners II, took off. Thanks to the help of Major, European heavy hitters, like Credit Lyonnais, Commerzbank, and Credit Agricole, contributed to the fund. As did American heavies, like AIG Global Investment, AMR Investment Services, BankAmerica, and the World Bank pension fund. (Afsaneh Mashayekhi Beschloss, then treasurer and chief investment officer at the World Bank, was the woman in charge of pension fund investments. After she retired from the World Bank, having committed an undisclosed sum of money to Carlyle, she took a job with Carlyle, a trend that would be repeated through Carlyle's history. That is not to say that Carlyle promised anyone they did business with a job, but the regularity of deals that look like quid pro quo is alarming.) The money rolled in yet again, and by late summer in 1998, the company had doubled its initial goal for its second consecutive fund, closing it at $1.1 billion. It seemed as if Carlyle could do no wrong.

But they didn't stop there. Over the next two years, the company would raise funds for investments in Asia, begin marketing funds to Latin America and Russia, and start up several venture capital funds aimed at smaller investments of up-and-coming companies. It would set up real estate funds in Europe and the United States. By the end of the decade, Carlyle stood with more than a dozen funds and close to $10 billion under management. It was officially a juggernaut, and the world was taking notice. The company was hiring politicians from all over the world to further their cause: former president of the Philippines Fidel Ramos; Prime Minister of South Korea Park Tae-joon; former SEC Chairman Arthur Levitt. And, of course, George Bush Sr.

In the way that money breeds more money, Carlyle was becoming an unstoppable force during the latter half of the 1990s. Both the money and the talent that was pouring in was building something that transcended a traditional private equity firm. In fact, it transcended traditional business. Carlyle was transforming into an entirely new kind of company, unique in both its makeup and its approach to business. With all of the politicians now on board, Carlyle was far more powerful than other investment banks. It had an enormous amount of money and clout, both of which had a certain snowball effect that led the company into uncharted waters. But there was even more good fortune ahead. Much more.

10

BUYING BUSH

*The shady world of bribes, kickbacks, and
improper campaign contributions.*

—*Harper's Magazine,* "Notes on a Native Son,"
an article on the Bush campaign, February 2000

Cast of Characters

George W. Bush   President of the United States of America.

Paul Silvester   Former Connecticut State Treasurer.

Wayne Berman   Washington insider, financial backer of George W.
Bush, president of Park Strategies.

Denise Nappier   Connecticut State Treasurer.

Thomas Hicks   Founder of Hicks, Muse, Tate & Furst, Texas billionaire, Bush backer.

James Baker III

George W. Bush is a president who has long been criticized for
being beholden to corporate interests. And perhaps no company holds more sway over the president than the Carlyle Group.
After all, George W. Bush owes his presidency to two men: his
father, who provided him the Bush surname and his legacy of
success; and James Baker III, the man who first helped Bush Sr.
get elected president, then fought in the trenches of the Florida
recount to capture the 2000 election for his son. Both of those
men work for the same company: the Carlyle Group.

George W. Bush becoming the president of the United States would turn out to be a major boon to Carlyle's business. This was an eventuality that was not lost on Carlyle's executives during the younger Bush's campaign for the presidency, and as a result, Carlyle and its partners played as large a role as anybody in securing Bush's victory in 2000. But the road to the Bush White House was fraught with land mines for Carlyle. As Bush campaigned, the press examined his and his father's relationship to Carlyle, and the result was a series of stories about dubious investments, seemingly crooked kickbacks, and near-miss scandals, any one of which, had they hit their mark, could have brought Carlyle crashing back down to earth. Instead, as it had done so many times before, Carlyle deftly traversed the tricky terrain and reached the Bush White House relatively unscathed.

A Bush Bonanza

While Carlyle had amassed a formidable employee roster by the late 1990s, it wasn't until George W. Bush's announcement of his intent to run for president in 2000 that the full potential of the Carlyle arsenal began to dawn on the rest of the world. After all, it was Carlyle that had placed young Bush on the board of Caterair when he needed to beef up his business resume (though he would later eliminate any reference to the disastrous Caterair debacle in his official bio). And it was Carlyle who had been paying the senior Bush to give speeches and meet with foreign leaders around the world on their behalf. And then there was the host of former Reagan-Bush stalwarts, like Baker, Darman, and Carlucci, now on board at Carlyle. With billions already under management, funds closing at twice their initial targets, and a growing international profile, the prospect of George W. Bush becoming president on top of all that seemed unjust. After all, how was anyone in the private equity world going to compete with them now?

But that's exactly how things were setting up for the boys at Carlyle. Not ones to leave anything to chance, Carlyle did what they could to ensure their desired outcome to the 2000 elections. The company was among the top political contributors in the defense industry in the 2000 election cycle. According to the Center for Responsive Politics, Carlyle contributed more than $427,000 to political candidates in 2000. A total of 84 percent of those contributions went to Republicans, making Carlyle the most partisan of the top 10 defense contributors. George W. Bush received more than $190,000 in campaign contributions from defense contractors in 2000, more than four times the amount Democratic presidential nominee Al Gore received.

While the tantalizing prospects of one of their own setting up shop in the White House filled their dreams, the campaign of George W. Bush cast an unwanted light on the connections that Carlyle had cultivated over the previous decade. And the resulting investigations by the press would add to the public's suspicions of the Carlyle Group.

Close Call in Connecticut

It all started off innocently enough. The news that Connecticut's former state treasurer was under investigation for investing the state's pension fund without proper due diligence barely caused a stir in New England, let alone Washington. Things like this happened all the time. And the situation in Connecticut looked relatively harmless as compared to other pension fund scandals. He probably just made a few bad investments. Didn't do his homework. Nothing to get too upset about.

But gradually the story started to take on a life of its own, and it became clear that this was not your run-of-the-mill negligence. This was something far more sinister. Over time, the complicated web of bribes and kickbacks was uncovered, and the result was the Carlyle name getting dragged through the mud again.

After he lost his bid for reelection to the Connecticut State Treasurer's office in November 1998, but before he left office in January 1999, Paul J. Silvester was a busy man. He invested $800 million in state pension funds in a series of eleventh-hour placements during those two frenetic months. This inordinate amount of action for a lame-duck treasurer raised eyebrows at the FBI, and the Bureau began an investigation. The Bureau wanted to know where the money had been placed, and why Silvester was in such a hurry to invest it. Silvester told the press that there was nothing irregular about the investments, and the whole thing was nothing but "a politically motivated witch hunt," contrived by one of his former political rivals. Nevertheless, Silvester resigned his newly acquired position at an investment firm called Park Strategies to concentrate entirely on the investigation. His new boss at Park Strategies, Wayne Berman, told the press early on that Silvester "resigned for personal reasons." It was one of the last times Berman would talk to the press on the matter.

But the investigation turned when agents realized that at least two of the investments that Silvester had made during the period in question were placed through Park Strategies, the same firm that had hired Silvester upon his leaving the state treasury. It worked like this: Silvester landed a high-level position at Park Strategies almost immediately after placing the investments and leaving office. On the face of it, it appeared as if Silvester was securing his future by investing the money through Park Strategies, which in turn had agreed to hire him.

Incidentally, Park Strategies placed $50 million of the money that Silvester invested into an Asian buyout fund run by Washington, DC's most connected company: The Carlyle Group. By the summer of 1999, the focus of the investigation shifted onto whether Silvester had shuttled the money through Park Strategies in return for getting a job. The fact that the money had ended up with Carlyle seemed irrelevant. But every week, media scrutiny on Wayne Berman increased. Park Strategies LLC was a consulting firm that Berman set up with former U.S. Senator Alfonse D'Amato, a Republican from New York. Berman worked in the first Bush administration's Commerce Department and was also one of the largest fund raisers to the George W. Bush campaign, having raised more than $100,000 for the cause. He was thoroughly connected in DC.

Soon, the focus of the investigation again shifted. The FBI now wanted to know if Silvester had received illegal kickbacks, either from Berman or his clients like the Carlyle Group, in exchange for his placement of the $800 million, of which $50 million went to Carlyle. Federal officials subpoenaed information from Park Strategies and Carlyle, as well as dozens of other investment firms. Homes were searched, files were confiscated, and dozens of interviews were conducted as part of the investigation. And finally, Silvester cracked. On September 23, 1999, Paul Silvester pleaded guilty to charges of corruption. Over the ensuing months, a complicated ring of kickbacks would result in fines and indictments for several of Silvester's family members, including his brother and brother-in-law. Together, the Silvester family had been accepting bribes for years, buying themselves boats and shiny new coats of paint on their houses.

Many of the documents from the case remained sealed, but the *Hartford Courant* quoted court documents that explicitly said Silvester "understood that his employment opportunity and/or substantial salary was contingent on his investing Connecticut state pension money with" a particular fund, referred to ambiguously as "Fund No. 4." The newspaper also reported that Berman had received fees, as much as $1,000,000, by virtue of Silvester's investments with Carlyle. Berman says the number was closer to $900,000. Finder's fees are not illegal, and though unusual, they are not unheard of. The concern is they can sometimes be used illegally as quid pro quo in kickback deals.

To this day it is not clear which fund the court documents are referring to. According to Bernard Kavaler, director of communications at the Connecticut Treasury Department, the U.S. attorney's office has not named the firms involved because the case is still pending. Paul Silvester has yet to be sentenced, though he is spending his days in jail. "They used letters and numbers in the court documents," Bernard Kavaler told me in September of 2002. "They still haven't named the who's who yet." In the meantime, the public is left to speculate.

As a result of the added scrutiny, Berman suspended his fundraising activity for George W. Bush. Berman maintains his innocence on any and all accusations to this day and calls the whole mess "ancient history." He went on to tell me that "the only thing I suffered from in this was some bad publicity from a 50,000 circulation newspaper. It all just evaporated. Everything I did was aboveboard." Berman told me that after the U.S. attorney's office requested some paperwork from him, which he provided, they never again contacted him on the matter. "I was never interviewed, they never called, never sent me a letter, never sent me a birthday card. I was never questioned. It is fair to say, therefore, they didn't think I did anything wrong."

On September 30, 1999, the new treasurer in Connecticut, Denise Nappier, called for new disclosure standards for Connecticut and asked that all recipients of state investments reveal to whom they had paid finders' fees. She also announced that she would make the findings public. The idea was to make investment banks more accountable for their behavior, be it legal or illegal. Following are excerpts from the first letter from Nappier to Rubenstein:

Dear Mr. Rubenstein:

As part of an ongoing federal investigation, the United States Attorney for the District of Connecticut recently disclosed a series of improper and illegal activities engaged in by my predecessor, Paul J. Silvester.

The information detailed by the United States Attorney focused, in part, on improper use of finder's fees. While it is my understanding that use of such fees can, in certain circumstances, be a legitimate business practice, the federal investigation has raised a myriad of legal and ethical issues, including possible and probable conflicts of interest and appearances of impropriety. In our effort to comply with the spirit and letter of all Connecticut and federal laws, and consistent with my long-standing interest in public disclosure, it is necessary that we formally ask all firms and individuals doing business with the Office of the State Treasurer to disclose finder's fees or other compensation paid to anyone as a part of any transaction related to the introduction, award, or continuation of business with my Office.

Accordingly, I request that you provide, on the forms enclosed herewith, a detailed disclosure of any and all finder's fees, placement fees, consulting contracts, or other compensation currently made in connection with any transaction or ongoing arrangements related to procuring or doing business with the Office of the State Treasurer, as well as any such arrangements during the past five (5) years. As part of this disclosure, I ask that you identify the individuals or entities receiving any such compensation and the amount of each payment. In the event that your company did not pay finder's fees, placement agent fees, or furnish other compensation at any time during this period, kindly so indicate in your response.

Please forward your response on *or before October 15, 1999,* to the attention of Catherine E. LaMarr, Esq., General Counsel, Office of the State Treasurer, 55 Elm Street, Hartford, Connecticut 06106-1773.

My office values our relationships with each of our vendors, and we appreciate your prompt and careful attention to this matter.

Sincerely,

Denise L. Nappier
State Treasurer

Hundreds of funds, fearful of losing Connecticut's business, complied with Nappier's requests immediately. But Carlyle's disclosure for its Asia fund was unacceptable by Nappier's standards, and the company outright declined to submit a report on its European fund, which Silvester had also invested in during his tenure as treasurer.

Nappier, her patience wearing thin, then sent another letter to Carlyle, more than a month after the first, threatening to cease all business dealings with the firm if they refused to disclose their finder's fees.

Dear Mr. Rubenstein:

By letter dated September 30, 1999, I requested that your company voluntarily disclose all compensation paid or promised in connection with any transaction or ongoing arrangements related to procuring or doing business with the Office of the State Treasurer since January 1, 1995. To date, we have not received a response to this request.

Disclosure of this information is the policy of this administration. Failure to comply will certainly jeopardize your company's current business relationship with the Office of the State Treasurer, as well as any prospects for future business.

In the event that we do not receive a full and complete response by the close of business on November 15, we will work with Connecticut's attorney general to pursue every legal recourse available to suspend or end our business relationship with your firm.

Sincerely,

Denise L. Nappier
State Treasurer

More than a month had passed since Nappier's original request and still nothing from Carlyle about their European fund. The *Wall Street Journal* reported on September 29 that Nappier was already starting the process of unwinding or canceling $561 million in investments made under her corrupt predecessor, including money invested with Carlyle. The clock was ticking, and there was $150 million at stake for Carlyle. It appeared as if Carlyle did not want the public to know something. Why else risk losing the money?

Finally, Carlyle came clean, delivering a full report to Nappier and the state of Connecticut. The company said that it had paid Wayne Berman a $1 million finder's fee for a $100 million placement from the Connecticut State Pension Fund into the Carlyle European Partners fund. In addition, the Associated Press reported in January 2000 that the Connecticut State Treasurer's office had paid a whopping $2,971,945 fee to Carlyle Europe Partners, the nature of which remains unclear to this day.

More Money, More Problems

The Silvester case was a close call for Carlyle, and the company's profile was becoming a little too pronounced for Rubenstein and company. It wasn't just the Silvester scandal that was turning up the heat however. George W. Bush's campaign for president had the press in overdrive, digging voraciously into the younger Bush's past, looking for examples of corporate cronyism, nepotism, shady dealings—anything that would sell newspapers. Democrats were eager to portray Bush as the "corporate candidate," or "Daddy's little boy." With Carlyle, both the media and Bush's opposition thought they had found something. They were asking copious numbers of questions. Who was this secretive company that Bush Sr. was working for? Aren't there some conflicts of interest inherent in this arrangement? Just how much business has George W. Bush done with the Carlyle group?

As it turned out, the Silvester affair led reporters to another questionable association between George W. Bush and big business, and once again Carlyle found itself running for cover. Enterprising young reporters were more interested in establishing the elusive connection between Berman's dealings with Silvester, and his generous campaign contributions to Bush. It was a connection they failed to establish. But the hunt for questionable campaign contributions led them to another financial supporter of Bush: Tom Hicks.

In February 2000, *Harper's Magazine* wrote an epic piece laying out the George W. Bush's business history in excruciating detail. It scrutinized the relationship between Bush and Thomas O. Hicks, a self-made Texas millionaire whose company, Hicks, Muse, Tate & Furst, was among Carlyle's biggest competitors in the private equity business. Hicks, a dedicated Texas Longhorns fan, had been up for a seat on the University of Texas' board of regents when George W. became governor in 1994. With the transition in power in Austin threatening his promised seat, Hicks provided Bush with a $25,000 campaign contribution, after he'd already won the election. Some say contributing to a campaign after the campaign is already over is another way of giving free money to a politician in return for a favor. And Bush did push through Hicks' coveted appointment to the board. Favor granted?

Through his new position, Hicks encouraged the University to more aggressively invest its $13 billion in financial assets, which includes endowments, donations, alumni contributions, and so on. Frustrated with the conservative strategy of years past, Hicks felt the University was leaving money on the table and had big ideas on how to change that. The answer was the P-word: *privatization*. Hicks fought hard to create a private company through which the assets of the University of Texas would be managed. It was a bold strategy, but one that fit with the larger trend toward privatization sweeping the nation.

By 1996, University of Texas Investment Management Company (UTIMCO) was born. Tom Hicks was quite pleased with the creation of UTIMCO, but the public and press were a bit miffed. As it turned out, the nonprofit company no longer had to divulge details on the investments of the University's money to the public; due diligence reports were not made available to the press. No one knew what the University's money was being spent on anymore. It was an untenable situation for the University's investors. But it went on for years.

Over time, the press and political action committees forced UTIMCO to open up its books, for fear that investments were being made based on political leanings and personal relationships. They found what they had suspected. Among the reams of Republican-friendly recipients of investments was, perhaps not surprisingly, the Carlyle Group. Weeks after Bush became governor in 1994, the University's board of regents placed $10 million into Carlyle Partners II, the fund that holds the bulk of the company's defense investments, as well as the lion's share of its controversy. It was a stunning example of how big business and politics are never far apart. Tom Hicks, an appointee of George W. Bush, had helped place $10 million of the University's money with a firm that not only had employed George W. a year earlier (via Caterair), but at the time was also considering employing George H. W. Bush. It was classic Carlyle, commingling business and politics to the point that the lines are blurred.

Hicks told *Harper's* that he didn't know of the relationships within the Carlyle Group when he made the investment. In fact, he went on to say that he suspected internal problems within the firm (most likely the ongoing feud between Norris and Conway) and had reservations about the investment from the onset. Which begs the question: Why invest in them at all? Especially in light of the fact that Carlyle is the supposed competition to Hicks, Muse, Tate & Furst. Tom Hicks, like so many others that do business with Carlyle, declined to be interviewed for this book.

It appears that UTIMCO's investments were at least partially politically motivated, rather than purely financially motivated. And that is the power of Carlyle. When an investor commits capital to a Carlyle fund, are they making a sound financial investment or a strategic political contribution? The inherent confusion works to Carlyle advantage.

Baker's Battle

Many political experts thought that the revelations about Berman and Hicks would do serious damage to George W. Bush's presidential campaign. It's impossible to know just how much of an effect the news had on voters. But however great the damage was, it paled in comparison to the value of the money that Berman and Hicks would contribute to Bush's campaign over time. Miraculously, Carlyle managed to tiptoe through the landmines relatively unscathed, aside from some unwanted attention. However, speculation over Carlyle's political leanings and what the company had or had not done to further George W. Bush's political aspirations became a moot point when James Baker got a call from Bush's campaign manager the day after the 2000 presidential elections: He was needed in Florida.

From the moment he was called into duty on November 8, 2000, until the day that Gore conceded the election on December 13, Baker dedicated himself tirelessly to winning the Florida vote for Bush. Having sat out the previous two campaigns, including

George W. Bush's, Baker jumped into the fray with both feet. It was obvious he hadn't lost a step.

After taking a plea for help from Bush's campaign manager, Baker flew to Florida immediately to assess the situation. So many things were riding on this vote. Baker, already as partisan a politician as there is, had many reasons to want the younger Bush in office. For one, there was the eight long years he had spent in exile since the Clinton administration took office. The hatred that Republican stalwarts harbored for Clinton and Gore cannot be overstated. Then, there was Baker's fierce loyalty to his close friends in the Bush family. And finally, the new life that Baker had carved out for himself since leaving the public's eye— that of a lawyer at Baker Botts and a globe-trotting deal maker for Carlyle Group—would benefit substantially if a close family friend were in office. The motivation was stacked.

Baker brought the same tenacity into Florida that he brought to his previous five Republican presidential campaigns. He relentlessly went to work attacking the Gore camp's motto, repeated ad nausea during the fight for Florida, of "Count all the votes." Baker was quoted in Jeffrey Toobin's definitive book on the subject, *Too Close to Call: The Thirty-Six Day Battle to Decide the 2000 Election,* as saying, "We need a PR strategy, we're getting killed on 'Count all the votes.' Who the hell could be against that?" Republicans, that's who. Baker wanted to limit the amount of votes that were recounted, knowing that with Bush already in the lead, the fewer votes that are recounted, the better Bush's chances of winning. Recounting them all could only lead to bad things.

But the Gore camp decided not to get too greedy by asking for a full recount throughout the state. Instead, they asked for a selective recount, only in the most controversial counties. Gore's people thought the tactic would be seen by the public as generous and fair, but they forgot that the campaigning was over, and the public's impression no longer mattered.

Baker turned the tables on Gore, filing a federal lawsuit claiming that the Gore camp's selective recount request only included counties in which Gore was likely to pick up votes. Many of the lawyers at work with Baker felt filing a lawsuit would look bad, and ultimately be a losing strategy. But Baker knew better. It was a litigious long shot, and ironically opposed their real goals. The fact of the matter was that the Baker/Bush camp had no intention of recounting all of the votes. They didn't want any of the votes recounted. As far as they were concerned, they had already won the election.

Baker carried out the operation in Florida with military precision. He spoke to George W. Bush often, sometimes four times a day. Though Baker kept Bush informed, he was in no way taking orders from the much younger presidential candidate. Baker was in complete command, calling all the shots. He managed to somehow sway the opinion of the court and Florida lawmakers against a recount, painting Gore as a sore loser, desperate to gain an edge. He held press conferences, claiming to be acting to "preserve the integrity and the consistency and the equality and the finality of the most important civic action that Americans take: their votes in an election for the president of the United States."

Over time, Baker developed an overused mantra of his own: The vote in Florida was counted and recounted, referring to the automatic recount of machine ballots. This was a claim, which Toobin points out, was entirely untrue. The automatic recounts that took place in Florida simply rechecked the totals that machines had spit out. It did not put the ballots through the machines again, the true meaning of a recount. Eighteen counties failed to properly recount their votes, accounting for more than a quarter of the total votes cast. Yet Baker managed to make Gore look like a fool for asking for "third" and "fourth" recounts. It was a brilliant strategy. And it worked.

The public relations battle in hand, Baker turned his attention to the legal arguments. The Gore camp never had a chance. Baker assembled an army of high-powered lawyers and political operatives, spread them around the state and country, and summarily eviscerated the Gore camp, which was led by Warren Christopher, no slouch in his own right. It was Baker at his very best: relentless, merciless, and victorious. On December 13, Gore conceded and George W. Bush became the forty-third president of the United States.

So much of what the Carlyle Group had done to this point in their history was setting them up for this moment: the defense investments, the extensive interests in the Middle East, the Republican administration in exile. Though the company would lose some of their most useful advisors and friends to the Bush White House staff, like Colin Powell, who became secretary of state, and Donald Rumsfeld, who became secretary of defense, they knew their buddies would not be far away. In fact, they would be right down the street. And even more useful than ever.

11

FAMILY BUSINESS

To this day we don't understand why [George H. W. Bush]
hasn't resigned. It's causing a scandal.

—Tom Fitton, Judicial Watch,
in a phone interview, November 2001

Cast of Characters

William Kennard	Former chairman of the Federal Communications Commission (FCC), Carlyle director.
Frank Yeary	Former investment banker at Salomon Smith Barney, Carlyle director.
Arthur Levitt	Former chairman of the Securities and Exchange Commission (SEC), Carlyle advisor.
George Herbert Walker Bush	Former president of the United States of America, Carlyle advisor.
Park Tae-joon	Former prime minister of South Korea, Carlyle advisor.
Michael Kim	Son-in-law of Park Tae-joon, Carlyle managing director.
Crown Prince Abdullah	Heir to the Saudi Arabian throne.
Tom Fitton	President, Judicial Watch.

Merriam Webster's Dictionary defines *nepotism* as a noun, meaning favoritism based on kinship. It is a simple definition, inherently neutral, and easy to understand. After all, isn't it natural to favor your own family members over strangers? It seems harmless enough. But when applied to international politics, it could not be more inappropriate. Our world leaders have a responsibility to act on behalf of the people they represent. Many of them take an oath to that effect. So when a politician, particularly the president of the United States, demonstrates nepotism in his actions, it is cause for serious and immediate alarm. George Herbert Walker Bush and his son George W. Bush have repeatedly and flagrantly crossed this border of impropriety since the younger Bush became president in 2001. And the company creating this ongoing breach of the public's trust is the Carlyle Group.

Money: A Bi-Partisan Goal

The ascension of George W. Bush to the presidency wasn't all good for the Carlyle Group. It was true that the new president had close ties to the company and would be in a position to send all kinds of business their way. It could even be said that the new president might be inclined, or at least not disinclined, to push policies and projects that might fatten his father's, and in a less direct way his own, bank accounts. But along with those newfound advantages for Carlyle came the continued, and at times increased, scrutiny of its behavior; fevered charges of cronyism; and the occasional accusation that the company was not a private equity firm at all, but rather a shadow government pulling the strings in Washington. Some of these concerns are more legitimate than others, but there was another more immediate issue: Who were they going to hire now that all the Republicans were going back to work?

Carlyle had been cultivating an unseemly reputation as a Republican boys club, whose membership privileges included the thrill of deal making on a global scale and a hefty paycheck at the end of the month. Indeed, it was difficult to spot any Democrats on the employee roster aside from Rubenstein himself, and he was 20 years removed from service by this time. But as always,

Carlyle already had a plan. It was time once again to pick over the bones of an outgoing administration. And this time, they were looking to harvest a host of Democrats.

In the spring of 2001, just a few months after Clinton had cleared out his desk, Carlyle snatched up both outgoing Federal Communications Commission (FCC) chairman William Kennard and outgoing Securities and Exchange Commission (SEC) chairman Arthur Levitt. The announcements of their hirings were less than a week apart. Both men are loyal to traditional democratic doctrine. Levitt has long been known for his concern for the individual investor, fighting to defend the little guys from the scourge of corporate greed. In one master stroke, indeed in one week, the Carlyle Group went from being a dark and mysterious GOP lair to a bright and open bipartisan buyout firm with a heart. It was Rubenstein at his best, fully aware of public opinion, and ready to make whatever changes were needed. Incidentally, the company had also picked up two of the best minds in the telecommunications and securities businesses.

But like most of Carlyle's high-profile hires, it seems that Kennard and Levitt did not come without baggage.

Over the course of 2000, SBC Communications, the parent company of the Baby Bell Southwestern Bell, was pursuing two major agendas simultaneously. On one hand, SBC was eager to buy into the Saudi Telecommunications Company (STC), as the Saudi Arabian Kingdom took the state-owned and run telephone monopoly private. In so doing, the company had briefly partnered with Carlyle to help them, because, as one European investor noted, "Carlyle had Saudi Arabia completely sown up. They controlled the deal flow in and out."

Two years earlier, Carlyle had hired Frank Yeary, former head of the media and telecommunications investment group at Salomon Smith Barney. With Salomon, Yeary had helped SBC grow from a thriving regional telephone company into the second largest telecommunications firm in the country by acquiring

Ameritech and Pacific Telesis. Then in 1998, he had helped Carlyle and a partner buy some cable properties in Virginia and Maryland from SBC for $250 million, then turn around and sell them six months later to Comcast for $735 million. He was a legend in telecom. And he was very close to the folks at SBC. Carlyle was in the perfect position to facilitate the deal in Saudi Arabia, which they did, extremely quietly, in August 2000. The deal was so secretive, it was near miraculous that anybody got wind of it at all. But an Arabic daily called *Asharq al-Awsat* reported that the Saudi government had chosen SBC Communications to buy between 20 percent and 40 percent in the Saudi Telecommunications Company, which had an estimated value of $12 billion at the time. The deal was termed a "strategic partnership." Any number of telecom companies would have wanted in on it, but with Carlyle on its side, SBC never had any real competition. (Ultimately, the deal fell through at the eleventh hour.)

At the same time, SBC was chaffing under newly established restrictions on telecommunications companies at home in the United States. Under the Telecommunications Act of 1996, regional bell operation companies, or Baby Bells, had to make their local lines available to the national long distance companies before they would be able to enter the long distance market themselves. Baby Bells, by nature of the telecommunications structure in the United States, had been government sanctioned regional monopolies since Ma Bell was broken up. Each Baby Bell owned and operated all of the local telephone lines for a given geographic area. Like Bell Atlantic in the Northeast, Pacific Bell in California, or Southwestern Bell in Texas. But the Telecommunications Act of 1996 was supposed to change all of that, opening up each region to competition. The tricky part was ensuring the Baby Bells would allow new competitors in to use their lines, thereby taking customers away. A bureaucratic nightmare of line request forms, fees, and fines for noncompliance emerged. Not surprisingly, new competitors had an impossible time securing lines from the Baby Bells, who protected their turf with arrogance and defiance of the new law. It was a mess.

Baby Bells, like SBC, abused the spirit of the Telecommunications Act of 1996 repeatedly. When competitive local carriers requested lines for a new customer, the Baby Bells would drag their feet, with little or no incentive to help a new competitor steal their customers. The fines for this anticompetitive behavior, levied by the FCC, were nominal and harmlessly factored in as a cost of doing business by the Baby Bells. Many of the would-be competitors in local markets dried up and died waiting for lines they knew they would never get from the likes of SBC. SBC was among the biggest offenders, drawing millions in fines and testing the patience of regulators and potential competitors alike.

That's why jaws dropped when SBC filed an application to begin delivering long-distance service in Texas at the end of 1999. Competitors that had been trying to get a fair shake in Texas, waiting in vain to gain access to SBCs local lines, couldn't believe it. The law clearly stated that a Baby Bell must open its local lines up to competition before it would be allowed to enter the long distance markets. SBC had not done that yet. So the U.S. Department of Justice recommended in February of 2000 that the application be rejected on the basis that SBC had not sufficiently opened up its network to competitors. But the Department of Justice (DOJ) doesn't get the final say in the matter. The FCC, chaired by William Kennard, does.

SBC withdrew the application at the FCC's request, and reapplied a few months later. After being embarrassed by the original rejection, the company pointed to the recommendation of the Texas Public Utilities Commission (TPUC) to approve the application, which the DOJ had summarily dismissed. The TPUC, happens to be chock full of Bush appointees, and SBC was one of the largest single corporate contributors to Bush's presidential campaign. "What this sounds like is, [the DOJ] is telling the Texas state commission it doesn't know what it's doing," said Michael Balhoff, managing director at Legg Mason, in an interview with the *Houston Chronicle*.

To the shock and dismay of many, SBC's application was ultimately approved by William Kennard and the FCC in the summer of 2000, and SBC was free to deal long distance in Texas. And in January 2001, the FCC approved SBC's application to offer long distance in Oklahoma and Kansas as well, making it the first Baby Bell company to offer interstate service since the breakup of Ma Bell. The approval was handed down on Kennard's last day as FCC chairman. Less than five months later, Kennard was working alongside the boys at Carlyle. It was all sounding awfully familiar.

The hiring of William Kennard brought with it the same appearance of impropriety that the hiring of Frank Carlucci brought. It looked quite a bit like the hiring of Paul Silvester at Park Strategies after he left the office of the treasury of Connecticut, and that of Afsaneh Mashayekhi Beschloss after she left her post at the World Bank. Here were men and women that made industry-altering decisions while in powerful positions and public office, then put themselves in a position to profit from those decisions months after they left their posts. Kennard, along with the rest of Carlyle, declined to be interviewed for this book. He later strenuously denied any wrongdoing. Regardless, while the Kennard situation smells bad, there was, and still is, another problem that Carlyle has on its hands that has a much mightier stink.

That ex-presidents cash in on their celebrity after their careers as public servants is understood. Most erstwhile chiefs end up on the public speaking circuit, pulling down $100,000 a speech. Many set up charity organizations, dabble in the stock market, or play a lot of golf. But never has an ex-president had the opportunities that George H. W. Bush has, doing business with heavily regulated industries, subject to the whims of the country's commander-in-chief, who also happens to be his son. And we may never see such an extraordinary arrangement again.

Papa's Got a Brand New Gig

After George W. Bush's swearing in, the national media immediately picked up Carlyle's scent again. Though the press missed the ironies and improprieties of Levitt and Kennard, they seized on the mother of all impropriety: The Bush family stood to gain financially from policy decisions George W. made while in office. The *New York Times* finally got in on the game, writing a revealing article in March 2001, detailing the relationships between the current administration and the Carlyle Group. It was the first most people had ever heard of this company, and it scared the pants off of them.

In the article, Charles Lewis, the executive director of the Center for Public Integrity is quoted as saying:

> Carlyle is as deeply wired into the current administration as they can possibly be. George H. W. Bush is getting money from private interests that have business before the government, while his son is president. And, in a really peculiar way, George W. Bush could, some day, benefit financially from his own administration's decisions, through his father's investments. The average American doesn't know that and, to me, that's a jaw-dropper.

As a member of their Asian advisory board, Bush Sr. was visiting the Middle East, and in particular, Saudi Arabia, on behalf of the Carlyle Group. Photos taken of a meeting between Bush Sr.

and King Fahd started popping up all over the Internet. A natural confusion arose over the nature of Bush's visits to foreign dignitaries. Were the trips a form of commercial diplomacy? Were they social visits? Was the former president representing U.S. interests? Or was he just there on behalf of a moneymaking behemoth by the name of the Carlyle Group? The same questions arose in the United Kingdom over the actions of John Major, who accompanied Bush on the trips to Saudi Arabia.

Of greater concern was that Major and Bush Sr. were meeting with less savory characters than the royal family. They had been to see the bin Laden family, the wealthy relatives of a known terrorist (by this time Osama bin Laden was unambiguously viewed as a terrorist threat to the United States, and estranged from his family). It wasn't clear what either of the former world leaders were up to. And it was this confusion, on the part of both the public and foreign world leaders, that played to Carlyle's advantage. Carlyle repeatedly reaped the benefit of blurred boundaries, with foreign business owners and world leaders not knowing whether Bush Sr. represents American political interests or Carlyle's financial interests. That was, and still is, a very powerful tool for Carlyle. But while everyone was waiting for a conflict of interest to arise in the elder Bush's business with Saudi Arabia—as indeed it would later—the real controversy was happening half a world away, in the tiny peninsula off the Eastern coast of Asia: Korea.

Sowing Carlyle's Seeds in Korea

On May 27, 1999, former president George H. W. Bush touched down in Seoul, South Korea, for a whirlwind business trip. His visit was celebrated in Seoul, with newspapers hailing his arrival, excited about the possibility of American investment in Korea in the wake of the Asian economic crisis of 1998. He met with South

Korea's Prime Minister Kim Jong-pil, and president of the United Liberal Democrats party Park Tae-joon, a major political figure in South Korea who had been advising Carlyle since 1998. He also met with the chairman of South Korea's Financial Supervisory Commission, Lee Hun-jai, chairman of SK Telecom Choi Tae-won, and the president of a financially ailing Asian conglomerate called Halla. Again, it was classic Carlyle: a measured blend of business and politics that sufficiently blurred the boundaries between the two.

Carlyle's spokespeople, when questioned by the press about the impropriety of the senior Bush working for a defense contractor while his son is president, often retort by explaining that all the senior Bush does for them is make speeches about world events. They say his job is to pack the house, get the crowd excited, then step aside while Rubenstein pries open their wallets. But this trip to South Korea was much more than that. Bush Sr. wasn't just giving speeches to rooms full of investors; he was doing business, one on one, with CEOs and politicians. These were not motivational talks about global politics. This was business. And he was good at it.

Carlyle was really starting to get busy in South Korea now. That same spring, the company hired Michael Kim, a Harvard-educated native Korean, to open its brand new Seoul offices. Kim is the son-in-law of aforementioned Park Tae-joon. Carlyle and nepotism seemed to go hand in hand.

Immediately following Bush's visit, Korean newspapers lauded an announced $1 billion investment in the country by Carlyle, including a buyout of a division of Mando Machinery, a South Korean industrial firm, owned by Halla, the same company Bush Sr. had visited weeks earlier. Bush had been busy, and apparently, successful on his quick two-day trip to South Korea. Carlyle was in business on the peninsula.

Bush went on to tour Thailand, with former prime minister and Carlyle advisor Anan Panyarachun, spreading more of the good news that money from America was coming. But back in Korea, Michael Kim was working to put together another massive deal. This time Carlyle was looking to buy one of the few healthy banks left in Korea, KorAm Bank. Korea, like the rest of Asia, had suffered terribly from the economic crisis that swept through the continent in the late 1990s. Many of the country's banks had faltered and collapsed. But KorAm was an exception. It had taken some hits, like all businesses in Korea, but had remained solvent. The Korean government had a vested interest in keeping the firm in Korean investors' hands. But Carlyle had other ideas.

Carlyle gained approval for the buyout by the KorAm board, thanks to its high-powered connections with Park Tae-joon, who became prime minister of South Korea in January 2000 and lobbied on Carlyle's behalf. But when Park resigned just four months after taking office, amid allegations of corruption, Carlyle had lost its regulatory advantage. It was going to be difficult to get the government to approve the deal without Park Tae-joon's involvement. So the firm then struggled to get the deal, which was to be for a 40 percent stake in the bank, approved by Seoul's Financial Supervisory Commission, the chairman of which Bush had met with a year prior. Carlyle was slipping, losing their political edge because of the unexpected and unseemly departure of Park Tae-joon from politics. They were losing the deal.

But after some months in self-imposed exile, Park Tae-joon, still a popular figure in Korea despite the allegations of corruption against him, came through in the end, rising from the ashes and lobbying the key government officials to allow the deal to happen, according to press accounts of the deal. By the fall of 2000, Carlyle had won, snagging 40.7 percent of the bank for $450 million. Between Bush Sr. and Park Tae-joon, Carlyle had made all the right moves to get their business in Korea humming. After another purchase of a small telecommunications carrier called Mercury Telecommunications, Carlyle had invested close to a billion dollars into Korea's recovering economy. It was the best financial news Korea had seen in years, and it was largely Carlyle's doing. But the mirth would soon come to an abrupt halt.

A Foreign Policy Flop

When George W. Bush was sworn in to office in January 2001, everything changed suddenly and dramatically. One of the first things that young Bush did as president was call off the missile control talks that the Clinton administration had been conducting with North Korea for years. Bush revealed open hostility toward North Korea, calling it a rogue state that cannot be trusted. It was a stunning reversal of American policy, which heretofore had been to use diplomacy in mitigating North Korea's military aggression toward South Korea. And it was coming from a man that had virtually no experience in foreign affairs. The nation watched in disbelief.

Not surprisingly, the backlash from Bush's brash actions was felt far and wide. North Korea accused the United States of planting a "time bomb" in the midst of their fragile negotiations with South Korea. The South Korean government received Bush's actions as a rebuff to their safety, knowing that North Korea would be more inclined to attack without Washington's involvement. Kim Dae-jung, South Korea's president, was forced to turn to the European Union for help in filling the sudden gap the United States had created in the peace process between North and South Korea. He was also getting lambasted at home for not being on top of the situation in Washington.

Bush had made the South Koreans look bad, and undermined their safety, all with one fell swoop. Analysts speculated that Bush was motivated by his desire to create a national missile defense system, part of his campaign platform. If North Korea had no missiles to defend against, the thinking went, Bush's need for a missile defense system would evaporate. As absurd as it sounds, peace between North and South Korea, and between North Korea and the United States, did not further his broader agenda in the White House. Regardless of his rationale, he had created an international crisis on just his second month on the job.

This also threatened Carlyle's extensive investments in South Korea, which would plummet in value as instability in the region increased. The threat of war always sends local economies into a tailspin, much like America's economy since September 11. And Carlyle could kiss regulatory approval for future deals goodbye, with South Korean officials feeling slighted by the United States, and particularly George W. Bush. At first it seemed as if this was a rare case in which being associated with the Bushes was not going to work to the benefit of Carlyle. But that would not prove to be the case.

Adding to the disarray George W.'s stance toward North Korea was causing, the unionists at KorAm bank were starting to rebel against their new American owners, accusing Carlyle of being nothing more than a speculative investor that had already broken its promise not to intervene with management. Employee representatives at the company believed that Carlyle intended to restructure the company, probably threatening jobs. And the union was rallying against Carlyle. The situation was dire. Carlyle had just ploughed nearly $1 billion into South Korea, and the man they all thought would be so good for business, George W. Bush, was on the verge of screwing it all up. Something had to be done.

On June 6, Bush reversed course. In a statement, the president announced plans to resume negotiations with North Korea, essentially picking up where the Clinton administration had left off. Among the issues that the new administration would work on with North Korea was improving relations between North and South Korea. The sigh of relief could be heard around the world, and especially from Carlyle's offices on Pennsylvania Avenue and in downtown Seoul. Just like that, the situation was all better. But what could have created the sudden change of heart?

On June 10, 2001, just a few days after the welcome announcement by President Bush, the *New York Times* reported that the senior Bush had forcefully argued for his son to reopen negotiations with North Korea shortly before President Bush did just that. The article opened:

> In an effort to influence one of his son's most crucial foreign policy decisions, former President George Bush sent to the president through his aides a memo forcefully arguing the need to reopen negotiations with North Korea, according to people who have seen the document.

It was the first time that anyone had tangibly seen the influence of the father on the son. According to the article, Bush Sr. felt that his son was being unduly influenced by the Pentagon, and that he should adopt a more moderate stance toward the Korean peninsula. He also spelled out that the hard-line policy toward North Korea was undermining the government in South Korea, thereby hurting U.S. interests in North Asia.

White House spokesman Ari Fleischer confirmed the report in the *Times,* and told the press that the argument for reopening negotiations came originally from Donald Gregg, former ambassador to South Korea under the first Bush administration. Fleischer said that Gregg had sent a memo to the senior Bush, who then sent the memo to national security advisor Condoleeza Rice, who then passed along "the thoughts in the note" to the president. It was a way of watering down the connection between George W. Bush and his father, even though it has been widely reported that the two speak regularly. Nobody in the White House wanted the press to get the impression that senior Bush was directly influencing the president. That's probably why Fleischer's accounting of the events made so little sense. Why Bush Sr. would have to go through Rice to relay crucial information on foreign policy to his son, when he talks to him twice a week on the telephone, is anyone's guess.

Bush Sr. went on to do even more damage control, recording reassuring remarks on U.S. policy to be distributed among participants in a crucial meeting between South Korean President Kim Dae-jung and North Korea's leader, Kim Jong-il, on Cheju Island. It seemed the former president was everywhere at once, acting as counsel to his son, ambassador to Korea, and business-man for Carlyle. For a man that had supposedly retired from politics, Bush Sr. was awfully busy.

Bush of Arabia

The folks at Carlyle refuse to talk about how ex-president Bush is compensated for his work on their behalf. Former employees, however, say that he is invested in the funds that he helps raise and place. If that is the case, the senior Bush's involvement in foreign policy regarding South Korea is a clear conflict of interest. He stands to gain financially from decisions that he is urging his son to make. It doesn't get any more egregious than that. But the press missed the connection at the time. Indeed it was a difficult connection to make, given that Bush Sr.'s trips to Korea and his work on behalf of Carlyle was kept very quiet. Then another story hit the front pages. Bush Sr. was at it again.

This time the *New York Times* reported that in July 2001, just months after he had advised his son on North Korea, the elder Bush had placed a call to Crown Prince Abdullah of Saudi Arabia on behalf of his son, to reassure Saudi Arabia's leadership that his son's "heart is in the right place," when it comes to Middle East policy. The call was necessitated by the younger Bush, who had upset the Arabs with his one-sided approach to the Israeli-Palestinian conflict. And Daddy was again there to bail him out.

The report said "former President Bush said that his son's 'heart is in the right place' and that his son was 'going to do the right thing,' a Middle East diplomat said. A senior administration official said that the phone call, warm and familiar in tone, was designed to encourage Abdullah to think of the new president as having a grasp of the Middle East similar to that of his father. According to one of the accounts, President Bush was in the room when his father made the call."

The news was stunning, and it undermined the credibility of George W. Bush on foreign policy. Who was making the decisions in the White House? Why didn't Bush Senior run for president instead? But more than that, the news of Bush Sr.'s continued involvement in foreign policy was undermining the credibility of both Bushes ability to keep politics and family business apart. Like the situation on Korea, Carlyle's extensive business interests in Saudi Arabia and throughout the Middle East, were in grave danger if the younger Bush kept pissing off the royal family. So the Senior Bush needed to step in and preserve the relationship once again. It was testament to the sway ex-president Bush still held over foreign affairs. And it didn't look good.

The reports of Bush Sr.'s actions sent the Washington, DC–based public advocacy groups into a tizzy. Tom Fitton, general counsel of Judicial Watch, a conservative watchdog group in the Beltway, is beside himself to this day. "It screamed conflict of interest," he says. "We asked publicly that the senior Bush should step down. To this day we don't understand why he hasn't resigned. It's causing a scandal."

That Judicial Watch has called on Bush Sr. to resign from Carlyle is more telling than you might think. This is not your average, ultraliberal watchdog organization. Judicial Watch is a public interest group that was conceived during the Clinton administration as a way to monitor activities that diminish the public's trust in government. It is an extremely conservative group, designed originally to bring down a Democratic president that the group felt was corrupt. "The Clinton administration was the most corrupt in history," says Fitton. "He was a rapist who took money from the Chinese. But he's lowered the bar so far that there is an acceptance of this everyday type of corruption." Other watchdog groups had been howling at Carlyle's antics for years, but when Judicial Watch, which had a reputation as a Republican-friendly group, could no longer look the other way, Carlyle had to take notice. "We're a conservative group, but we're not Republican. The Carlyle Group has been very upset with us, but this is an extraordinary company, very unique," says Fitton. "They hire these people, and I don't think they hire them for their good looks. I'm sure it smarts for them to know that we have raised ethical concerns on the part of the president's father."

Fitton points out that not only has the former president been making investments for Carlyle and weighing in on foreign policy that directly affects those investments, but he is also privy to CIA briefings whenever he sees fit, referred to internally at the CIA as "President's daddy's daily briefing," a right that all ex-presidents maintain. And according to press reports, Bush Sr. still requests and receives CIA briefings often. Despite being 10 years removed from his presidency, Bush Sr. remains an extremely powerful and influential man. Imagine what a global enterprise, that does large amounts of business with arms contractors and foreign governments, could do with weekly CIA briefings. Or a company with the ability to influence foreign governments and global events. A company like that would have access information that would set it apart from any company to come before it. A company like that could be very successful. A company like that might look a lot like Carlyle.

12

BIG GUNS

Killing this killing machine won't be easy.
—*Wall Street Journal,* "Heavy Metal," May 5, 2001

Cast of Characters

General Shinseki	U.S. Army chief of staff.
George W. Bush	President of the United States of America.
Donald Rumsfeld	Secretary of defense.
Andrew Krepinevich	Executive director of the Center for Strategic and Budgetary Assessments, opponent of Crusader.
Milo Djukanovic	President of Montenegro.
Colin Powell	Secretary of state.
Frank Finelli	Retired Army colonel.
Frank Carlucci	

The part of Carlyle's business that has naturally attracted controversy over the years is its defense business. It makes sense. War, after all, is inherently controversial. It usually involves heated passions, covert strategy, and death on a large scale. So it's not entirely surprising that ordinary American citizens felt outrage at Carlyle's commingling of ex-politicos, guns, and money. The idealist in all of us wants to believe that war is an awful, but necessary, part of the human condition. We want to think that our nations enter reluctantly into battle, always as a last resort, after all other means of resolving conflict are exhausted. And we never want to believe that war, and the destruction and horror that accompany it, could ever be seen as a business. But it is true. At least the people profiting from these wars aren't the same elected officials that have led us into battle in the past and still hold sway over current decision makers in the White House and the Pentagon, right? Wrong.

Crusader's Crusade

By 2001, the world outside of Washington, DC, was becoming dimly aware of the Carlyle Group. People would chat about them casually at cocktail parties, noting the intimidating employee roster and joking about shadow governments and X-files episodes. But it was all speculation at that point. No one in the media had put together the apparent conflicts of interests the Bushes had cultivated in Korea and Saudi Arabia. Yet people had a vague and nagging notion that there was something wrong with the way Carlyle was conducting its business. They were just having trouble putting a name to it. Everyone was looking for the proverbial smoking gun. Little did they know that it was literally a smoking gun they would find.

The saga began in the summer of 1997, when Carlyle was raising money like mad, hiring world leaders, and, in general, becoming the dominating global private equity firm it is today. Among the investments Carlyle had targeted for its Carlyle Partners II fund—the one chock full of defense, aerospace, and security companies—was a maker of armored vehicles named United Defense. The owners of United Defense were FMC Corporation and Harsco Corporation—the same company that Carlyle had unsuccessfully and hostilely tried to acquire six years earlier. All Carlyle got for its $63 million back then was one lousy board seat with Harsco. But what a valuable board seat that had suddenly become.

The news around the defense industry August 1997 was that General Dynamics had bid $1 billion for United Defense, far more than any other bidder. General Dynamics already made armored vehicles, so United Defense's expertise—they made the Bradley fighting vehicles used in the Gulf War—fit perfectly with that of General Dynamics. The deal seemed like a no-brainer: highest bidder, synchronized interests, little overlap. There really was no competition. But at the last minute, Harsco and FMC decided instead to sell to the Carlyle Group, which had submitted a low-ball bid of $850 million, 15 percent less than General Dynamics had been offering. It turns out that rumors had begun to circulate around Washington, DC, that General Dynamics was going to run into antitrust issues. Eventually, the rumors grew so loud that General Dynamics was forced to back out of the bidding, and Carlyle was there to pick up the scraps. It was another stunning victory for Carlyle.

Despite paying a fire-sale price for United Defense, Carlyle was not without its challenges regarding the new acquisition. Since 1994, United Defense had been working on a massive gun: a mobile howitzer that can fire 10 rounds of 100 pound shells per minute, 25 miles in distance, cruise at 29 mph, and reload on the battlefield. The "Crusader" was the most advanced artillery system the U.S. Army had ever conceived. It is the kind of weapon that makes the United Stated unbeatable in large scale, open warfare, lobbing multiple shells at varying trajectories so that they rain down at their desired target at the same time. It is a fearsome weapon. A killing machine. It was also United Defense's future cash cow.

But times had changed considerably since Crusader was first conceived in the early 1990s. In fact, the very nature of war had changed and had left Crusader behind. The gun had two very serious problems: It was too big, and it was designed to fight a type of battle that no longer presented itself to the U.S. armed forces. The gun is so out of date, in fact, that according to a congressionally appointed independent National Defense Panel in 1997, which reviewed all of the military's ongoing weapons projects, the Crusader was a Cold War inspired weapon, rapidly approaching obsolescence due to a military trend toward swift deployment and agile forces. It was a gun designed to fight large scale, open field battles, the kind the United States had not fought since World War II. Unfortunately, for Carlyle, the damning report came out just a few months after the company had acquired United Defense.

The problem was that at 60 tons each—plus a supply vehicle that weighed an additional 50 tons—the Crusader was impossible to deploy quickly enough to hot spots around the world. It could not be airlifted by any of the massive cargo planes employed by the Army. And shipping Crusader would take too long to reach the ephemeral battles to which the Army had recently grown accustomed. The United States had learned that lesson the hard way, when it took more than a month to ship its Apache helicopters to the action in Kosovo in 1999, a conflict that lasted only 78 days total. The United States wasn't fighting long, drawn out land wars in Europe anymore, and Crusader's effectiveness for the new breed of fighting was being called into question.

"For the foreseeable future, no one is going to stand out in the open and fight the American forces," says Andrew Krepinevich, a member of the 1997 National Defense Panel that panned the Crusader and executive director of the Center for Strategic and Budgetary Assessments. "The U.S. will be fighting in more complex terrain, like mountains and cities, and in those areas there is not a lot of use for heavy artillery of this nature. The big challenges are how do you get there fast and how do you fight people that won't fight you out in the open." The panel recommended the Crusader program be dramatically scaled back, and some, including Krepinevich, wanted it canceled outright.

A cancellation of the Crusader program would have been catastrophic for United Defense. The company had just lost out on a crucial contract with General Dynamics to build tracked fighting vehicles for the army. It was a devastating loss, leaving Crusader as the saving grace for the company. Losing the Crusader contract, originally valued at $20 billion, would jeopardize the future of the company and would be a mighty hit to Carlyle's premier fund, Carlyle Partners II.

The momentum against the Crusader was building rapidly by the turn of the century, as more defense analysts recognized the importance of mobile armed forces that could be deployed instantly. When General Shinseki took over as U.S. army chief of staff in June 1999, he preached the gospel of a faster, lighter army in which the Crusader played no role. Even George W. Bush, when running for office, questioned the utility of the Crusader. In a campaign speech in 1999, Bush recognized the end of the Cold War as an opportunity to "skip a generation of technology." It was all part of an effort to build an army "not by mass or size, but by mobility and swiftness," according to Bush. The future of the Army was at hand, and almost everyone was on board but United Defense. The Crusader had become the poster child of the old, lumbering Cold War army. *Time* magazine said of the Crusader, "the kind of war it was meant to fight is already obsolete." The *Wall Street Journal* called it a "dinosaur."

By all accounts, the Crusader was headed for the scrap heap. But Carlyle was just getting started. The effort the company put forth to save their precious gun would illustrate exactly how the Iron Triangle of defense, government, and business work together to the benefit of all three. Carlyle had been built to prevail in situations like these, when the large amounts of money were riding on the decisions of a few men in public office. It was time to call in a few favors.

Slimming Down

In the fall of 1999, General Shinseki told United Defense that if they did not reduce Crusader's weight to under 42 tons, light enough to be transported on a C-17 cargo plane, he was going to kill the program. He gave the company three months. "We were given a bogey," says Doug Coffey, vice president of corporate communications for United Defense. "We were told that we had to be able to put any two of the Crusaders on a C-17, so you could take a complete system anywhere in the world."

United Defense worked furiously through the winter to meet the goal. They redesigned the engine, stripped armor, and reduced ammunition. They worked through the Thanksgiving and Christmas holidays. By 2000, they had made their designated weight: 42 tons on the button.

In the meantime, Carlyle and United Defense were waging a political battle for the Crusader. Shortly before Carlyle bought the company, United Defense organized a political action committee (PAC) through which the company would funnel contributions to key lawmakers. In the cycle leading up to the 1998 elections, United Defense made campaign contributions of only $49,500. But by 2000, under Carlyle's leadership, the company's PAC had spread around more than $180,000 to more than 70 senate and house members. The bulk of the company's largesse went to politicians on the house and senate arms committees. And often, a good deal of money found its way to the house and senate members whose districts were expected to participate in manufacturing the Crusader. It was also uncanny how United Defense planned to build manufacturing facilities for the Crusader in the backyards of key members of the arms committees, creating jobs and wealth that hadn't existed before. These are the kinds of things that get politicians reelected, and get businesses what they want.

Rick Santorum, a Republican senator from Pennsylvania, netted $10,000 from the United Defense PAC in 2000. York, Pennsylvania, is home to a United Defense manufacturing facility. Another manufacturing facility for Crusader was located in Minnesota, home of republican senator Rod Grams, who took another $10,000 from the United Defense PAC. Republican representative J. C. Watts of Oklahoma received $6,000 from the United Defense

PAC. Watts's corner of Oklahoma, which included Fort Sill, was targeted as a factory site for assembly of Crusader. Watts was also a member of the House Armed Services Committee. Carlyle was being thorough and strategic, and they were starting to make up ground. Reports of Crusader's death had in fact been greatly exaggerated.

When reporters question Carlyle representatives about the potential for people like Frank Carlucci to lobby his good friends in the Pentagon and the White House, they receive admonishments and are made to feel unpatriotic for even suggesting the thought. One *Los Angeles Times* reporter was excoriated by a Carlyle spokesperson, "I assure you [Carlucci] doesn't lobby. That's the last thing he'd do. You'd have to know Carlucci to know he'd never do that, and you'd have to know Rumsfeld to know it wouldn't matter." The company often aggressively defends itself from accusations that it lobbies or has any undue influence over key decision makers. But concentrating on whether Carlyle "lobbies" or not is a red herring argument, designed to lead reporters on a wild goose chase for the elusive definition of lobbying. Besides, according to official records, Carlyle does in fact lobby.

According to the Center for Responsive Politics, the Carlyle Group spent more than $1,200,000 in 2000 hiring lobbying firms to wage battle on Capitol Hill on behalf of United Defense. What Carlyle representatives are really saying when they assure the public they do not lobby is that their high-profile hires like Carlucci, Bush, and Baker don't personally register as lobbyists and work to drum up support for various programs. That, of course, is true. But to say that the Carlyle Group doesn't lobby is simply not true. Rubenstein, a former lawyer, has been playing a cat-and-mouse game of semantics with the press for years. Does the Carlyle Group register as lobbyists? No. Do they hire lobbying firms to do it for them? Yes. Do they influence key lawmakers and help shape policy? Of course they do. People like Carlucci don't need to lobby, in the traditional sense of the word. They already know the lawmakers involved in key decisions, and the lawmakers know them. There are memorandums and meetings. There are unspoken understandings that are reached over a drink and a wink. "It's impossible to say when people working for Carlyle are wearing more than one hat," Peter Eisner, managing director at the Center for Public Integrity, told me. It would be ludicrous to imagine George Bush Sr. fighting it out in the trenches with all the other registered lobbyists. But does George Bush Sr. have a say in policy decisions made by this White House? That much has already been proven.

Regardless of your definition of lobbying, in the case of the Crusader, Carlucci and his team did lobby, and they lobbied hard. According to the *Wall Street Journal,* Carlucci called Defense Undersecretary Jacques Gansler multiple times to have the program spared. The *Wall Street Journal* also reported that Carlucci called defense think tanks and pleaded with them not to write anything negative about Crusader. Carlyle hired recently retired senator Dan Coats and his former staffer, a retired army colonel named Frank Finelli, to start stumping for Crusader. In an interview, Greg McCarthy, a spokesperson for now retired representative Watts, said this of Carlyle and Finelli: "Carlyle's strength was within the DOD. As a rule someone like Frank Carlucci is going to be able to have access, and members of congress are going to have an open door to Frank. Without question, they have influence. But the fact that this is all known mitigates that influence to some extent. They are not able to hide. But they have other, less visible people. They have these staff types that are behind the scenes; they work in the dark. Guys like Frank Finelli who know everything about the army and about Capitol Hill."

One of the lobbyists who Carlyle hired to work congressmen on Crusader had this to say of Carlyle: "I felt that in this effort, they were like any other lobbying group, aside from the fact that they are not one. They have been able to reach into Congress, and there was a lot of contact with the Pentagon. They definitely influenced the decision-making process."

Lobbying laws in the United States are vague and ill defined. Lobbyists are required to register with the federal government and disclose their clients and the payment amounts publicly. But what exactly constitutes lobbying is much less clear. The formal definitions of lobby are: (1) to conduct activities aimed at influencing public officials and especially members of a legislative body on legislation; and (2) to attempt to influence or sway (as a public official) toward a desired action. By those definitions, contributing funds to various lawmakers, calling the defense undersecretary to plead for the Crusader, and hiring $1,200,000 of lobbying groups on United Defense's behalf would indeed be considered lobbying. It's hard to see what Carlyle did in this case as anything but lobbying.

What they did was save their precious gun. Between the slimming down of the gun, the massive lobbying effort, and the scaling back of the original order from 1,200 to 480, the Crusader survived. When Bush's proposed defense budget for 2002 was finally handed down in June 2001, it included funding for Crusader. It was nothing short of a Hail Mary pass with no time left on the clock for Carlyle. And within two months of the decision by Bush, the Carlyle took its first dividends from United Defense, a windfall of $289 million. The Crusader was saved for the time being, but opponents continued to fight to have the program cancelled. The raging debate would not be ultimately settled until long after September 11, 2001.

Documenting Carlyle's Access

The actions of the Carlyle Group in the fight to save the Crusader drew an enormous amount of unwanted attention to the firm. Though the company defended itself from claims of undue

influence, public advocacy groups were sure Carlyle had unmiti-
gated and unethical access to the highest ranks of government.
The problem was, proving those kinds of things was nearly impossible. Interested parties would have to tail Frank Carlucci for
months, and even then, all you would learn was whom he met
with and when, not what was said. It just wasn't the kind of thing
a reporter could spend time on. But then there was a break.

Judicial Watch, the public interest law firm that investigates
government corruption and repeatedly called for the resignation
of Bush Sr. from the Carlyle Group, has been using legitimate
and legal means to prove to the American public that the Carlyle
Group has the ability to access and influence key decision makers
in the current administration. By utilizing the Freedom of Information Act, a law that gives the right for all citizens to request
and receive information from the federal government, Judicial
Watch has been able to obtain a smattering of documents from
the Department of State and the Department of Defense that illustrate the sway Carlyle holds. Many of Judicial Watch's requests
were ignored or delayed indefinitely, heightening their suspicions
of foul play and forcing them to file a lawsuit against the state and
legal departments to obtain the requested documents. Finally,
they saw a few documents coming their way. But only a few.

Judicial Watch grew increasingly frustrated as they were consistently stonewalled in their requests. But even the limited documents that the state and defense departments did release show
the power, reach, and influence of Carlyle. The first documents
Judicial Watch received are correspondences between Carlucci
and William Perry, another former secretary of defense, and Carlucci's good friend Donald Rumsfeld, the current secretary of
defense. In the letter to Rumsfeld from Carlucci and Perry,
which is on Carlyle letterhead, the two former secretaries of defense urge Rumsfeld to heed the findings in a report the BENS
Tail-to-Tooth Commission wrote on reducing infrastructure

spending in the Pentagon. Both Carlucci and Perry served on the BENS Commission: The BENS Commission stands for the Business Executives for National Security, and the suggestion, as the letter shows, is to "cut the cost of defense infrastructure and re-invest in modernization and other priority programs."

> Dear Don,
>
> Thanks for lunch last Friday. It was great seeing you in such good spirits even if you are "all alone."
>
> We thought it useful to follow up on our discussions on the need for reductions in the infrastructure of the Department— and how that might best be done. Over the past three years, the two of us have served as senior advisors to the BENS Tail-to-Tooth Commission. We believe the Commission has addressed the most critical areas that must be tackled if we are to cut the cost of defense infrastructure and re-invest the savings in modernization and other priority programs.
>
> Because the "what to do" is so well known, the beauty of the Commission's report is not in the issues it identifies—rather, it is the focus on implementation, the "how to do it," that sets it apart.
>
> We have taken the liberty of enclosing copies of this package and would be happy to discuss it with you or your staff. Or, perhaps more helpful, we would be pleased to introduce to you, or to whomever you might designate, the Commissioners who put this effort together.
>
> Best Regards,
>
> Sincerely,
> Frank C. Carlucci
> William J. Perry

In Rumsfeld's response, the secretary is clearly amenable to Carlucci's suggestions. He even invites the two of them to come in and address the staff within the Pentagon.

Dear Frank and Bill,

My apologies for the delay in getting back to you on your letter of February 15.

There is no question but that we are going to have to tackle the infrastructure issue. I've been impressed with the BENS Tail-to-Tooth report, and congratulate you folks for good work. What I may do is ask the two of you to come in and meet with some of the key staff folks who are working on those types of things here in the department.

I will be back in touch with you. With my appreciation and best wishes.

Sincerely,

Donald Rumsfeld

The BENS Commission report showed that too much money was being spent on support, overhead, staff, and the like, while not enough was being spent on supporting combat forces. In other words, Carlucci was encouraging Rumsfeld to spend less on infrastructure, more on weapons and the like—the precise business in which Carlyle is so heavily invested. The mere fact that Carlucci could have such unimpeded access to such an important decision is disturbing enough, but the nature of their correspondence is wholly inappropriate, given the obvious financial benefit of Carlucci should Rumsfeld follow his advice. And sure enough, by July 2001, Rumsfeld's defense budget was incorporating the BENS Commission's suggestions. "BENS has long advocated cutting overhead," beamed BENS CEO General Richard D. Hearney in the *Aerospace Daily*. "We are pleased to see that Secretary Rumsfeld is taking this approach in transforming the Pentagon."

The second document that Judicial Watch obtained was a long, in-depth letter from Carlucci to brand new Secretary of State Colin Powell, sent on February 23, 2001. In it, the chairman of the Carlyle Group, again on Carlyle letterhead, lays out an extensive argument for the United States to support Montenegro's desire for independence from Yugoslavia. Montenegro is among the more outspoken republics in the formerly war-torn region of Yugoslavia.

After allying with the United States in isolating, and eventually removing Slobodan Milosevic, Montenegrin President Milo Djukanovic was now pressing his case for Montenegrin independence in the Balkans. The move was widely opposed by the international community, including the United States, because of fears that the move toward independence would again destabilize the region, which had been at war for years and had finally reached some semblance of peace. Djukanovic came to the United States to press his case in early February 2001 and was rebuffed by Secretary Powell in his request for a meeting. The Bush administration had taken a stand against Montenegrin independence, fearing it would in fact plunge the entire region back into war. Djukanovic did manage to meet, however, with Frank Carlucci of the Carlyle Group. And the following is Carlucci's plea to Colin Powell on Montenegrin independence:

Dear Colin,

We congratulate you on your great start as Secretary of State. We recognize that there is no shortage of serious issues seeking your attention, but one of the earliest will certainly be Montenegro's relationship to Serbia.

As you know, Montenegro is the last of the five original non-Serbian republics to press its claim for independence. President Djukanovic was in Washington recently, and I hosted a long and spirited talk for several of us with Djukanovic to discuss his thinking. . . .

Djukanovic struck us as determined to proceed to independence. . . . Djukanovic stressed that he planned to achieve independence democratically and nonviolently without destabilizing

the region. . . . He said he understood that the real issue behind the coolness of Washington and the Europeans toward
Montenegrin independence was not Montenegro itself but the
impact of independence on Kosovo. . . .

At the conclusion of the meeting, he asked that the U.S. return to the position that, while you prefer Montenegro to remain part of the FRY, if the process to independence is open
and democratic, the United States would accept it. On behalf of
Mort Abramowitz, Max Kampelman, Jeane Kirkpatrick, Richard
Perle, Steve Solarz, and Hal Sonnenfeldt, we believe this position makes good policy sense and would be prepared to discuss
it with you.

Best wishes,

Frank C. Carlucci
Chairman

Why Frank Carlucci, the chairman of a private equity firm,
would be meeting with leaders of war-riddled nations is anyone's
guess. It is easy to see how anyone would be confused as to what
role he has in Montenegro's independence. Is he acting on behalf
of the United States? Or as a Carlyle executive, since the letter is
on Carlyle letterhead and signed "Chairman." But it is even more
baffling why he felt it necessary to directly lobby the state department for support of Montenegro's independence in the first place.
Perhaps his thinking was that the more instability in the Balkans,
the more need for war and the more weapons that are sold. All of
which benefits defense contractors, like Carlyle. Although unsub-
stantiated, that could be the intent behind Carlucci's overtures to
Powell. Regardless, Powell's administrators had the good sense to
recommend against the inappropriate meeting, recognizing that
Carlucci would likely have more to talk about with Powell than just
Montenegro. In this memo, Powell's assistant offers the secretary
two potential replies to Carlucci. Powell's stamp and initials indicate his declining of the meeting.

To: The Secretary

From: EUR—James F. Dobbins

Subject: Response to letter from Frank Carlucci

Issue for Decision

- Whether to sign attached response to Frank Carlucci, who has written you regarding the Administration's policy toward Montenegro.

Mr. Carlucci wrote to you on February 23 regarding the Administration's policy toward the government of Montenegro, asking that you take a more forthcoming position on the issue of independence. . . .

 While there is no harm in such a meeting, I am not sure that it would be worth your time. The discussion at such a meeting would likely go beyond Montenegro. . . .

The few documents that Judicial Watch was able to recover show the extraordinary reach of Carlyle Group into the Bush administration. In addition to making these documents public on their Web site, www.judicialwatch.org, the organization has repeatedly called for the resignation of George Bush Sr. from Carlyle, at least while his son is president. Judicial Watch chairman and general counsel had this to say in the group's May 4, 2001, press release:

This is simply inappropriate. Former President Bush should immediately resign from the Carlyle Group because it is an obvious conflict of interest. Any foreign government or foreign investor trying to curry favor with the current Bush administration is sure to throw business to the Carlyle Group. And with the former President Bush promoting the firm's investments abroad, foreign nationals could understandably confuse the Carlyle Group's interests with the interests of the United States government.

He goes on to say, very presciently, "questions are now bound to be raised if the recent Bush administration change in policy toward Iraq has the fingerprints of the Carlyle Group, which is trying to gain investments from other Arab countries who would presumably benefit from the new policy." This press release was issued in May 2001, before the terror attacks on the World Trade Center and the Pentagon, and before President Bush began incessantly banging the war drum on Iraq.

By the summer of 2001, the public outcry against the Carlyle Group had seemed to reach a fever pitch. The *New York Times,* the *Washington Post,* the *Wall Street Journal,* and the *Los Angeles Times* had all written grim and damning accounts of the company's business dealings within the Iron Triangle, particularly around the Crusader. Photographs and news accounts of Bush Sr. visiting the Saudi royal family had graced the cover of the *New York Times,* outraging those who believed Saudi Arabia to be more of an enemy than an ally. These were all stunning realizations for the American public. But nothing would compare to what was to come, on the day the world was changed forever: September 11, 2001.

13

9/11/01

No one wants to be a beneficiary of September 11.
—Carlyle partner Bill Conway, *The Nation*,
"Crony Capitalism Goes Global," April 1, 2002

Cast of Characters

Shafiq bin Laden	Estranged half-brother of Osama bin Laden, family representative to Carlyle investments.
Basil Al Rahim	Former Carlyle employee, Middle East fund-raiser.
Cynthia McKinney	Former Democratic representative from Georgia.
Chris Ullman	Carlyle spokesperson.
Richard Conte	Vice president and treasurer of IT Group, a Carlyle company.
Paul Wolfowitz	Deputy secretary of defense.
Donald Rumsfeld	

September 11 changed everyone's life. It's that simple. The impact is still being felt around the world as economies buckle, war looms, and uncertainty accompanies every step we take. Few can look back at the events of that day and conclude that anything good came of the attacks. But the grim reality is that for some, the September 11 attacks were not all bad. In fact, some businesses stood to make a lot of money from what went on that fateful day. Vendors on New York City streets could not stock the shelves with Fire Department hats and t-shirts fast enough.

Tourism in lower Manhattan boomed during the cleanup as hordes of onlookers crowded the streets, hoping to get a peek at the gaping hole the attacks had left.

For most New Yorkers, the willingness to profit from the tragedy was shameful and embarrassing. But it was mere pennies compared to the millions that Carlyle would go on to make after the attacks.

An Extraordinary Day

The skies over Manhattan that morning were astonishingly blue. It was one of those rare days of late summer, not a single cloud in the sky, temperatures so mild and inviting, you almost didn't mind getting up and going to work. It was an election day in New York, but there was no discernible difference in the way the city went about its business, aside from the buzz on the local news stations. Trucks honked industrial-strength horns, echoing down canyons of steel and glass. Cabbies swerved and jerked their bright yellow Fords from stoplight to stoplight on rush hour streets. Businessmen sidestepped delivery men on frenetic sidewalks, everyone hustling, with somewhere important to be. And the sky, unambiguously blue, looked down silently at the city below.

At 8:43 A.M., American Airlines Flight 11 from Boston tore through the daily cacophony of New York, ripping a path down midtown Manhattan, roaring toward the north tower of the World Trade Center. Many in midtown would shrug off the incident, wondering why a jumbo jet was flying so low, and maybe speculating with a friend, but never suspecting the ultimate destination. It wasn't until the thick, dark stripe of smoke from the explosion billowed and writhed against the clear blue sky on the southern horizon, that most New Yorkers knew something was terribly wrong. In Manhattan, the avenues cut from north to south, in dead straight lines. People began gathering on street corners to peer down the long avenues and get a look at the smoke. Co-workers crowded around company television sets, watching with confusion and fear, as the single tower smoked and burned.

Less than 20 minutes later, as the city, thirsty for information, devoured live television news reports, United Airlines Flight 175, banking hard from the west, disappeared into the south tower of the World Trade Center amidst a ring of fire and smoke. News-casters were initially baffled, as if their networks had suddenly come across footage of the first plane hitting the tower. Suddenly the dreadful logic of what was unfolding quickly took hold, and the grim reality dawned on the city's collective conscience at once, with inescapable reality: It was a second plane, and we were under attack.

The fear that descended on the city was immediately palpable. Without speaking, everyone not directly involved in the horrifying events taking place at the Trade Center asked themselves the same questions: How long will this go on for? Is my building safe? Who do I know in the Twin Towers? Will God ever forgive us for this?

The city was instantaneously shut down. Bridges and tunnels were sealed off. Subways stopped running. Airplanes were redirected and landed at alternate airports. Then, at 9:43 A.M., American Airlines Flight 77 crashed into the Pentagon, leaving little doubt that the attacks were ongoing.

A Chance Meeting

That same morning, in the plush setting of the Ritz-Carlton hotel in Washington, DC, the Carlyle Group was holding its annual international investor conference. Frank Carlucci, James Baker III, David Rubenstein, William Conway, and Dan D'Aniello were together, along with a host of former world leaders, former defense experts, wealthy Arabs from the Middle East, and major international investors as the terror played out on television. There with them, looking after the investments of his family was Shafiq bin Laden, Osama bin Laden's estranged half-brother. George Bush Sr. was also at the conference, but Carlyle's spokesperson says the former president left before the terror attacks, and was on an airplane over the Midwest when flights across the country were grounded on the morning of September 11. In any circumstance, a confluence of such politically complex and globally connected people would have been curious, even newsworthy. But in the context of the terrorist attacks being waged against the United States by a group of Saudi nationals led by Osama bin Laden, the group assembled at the Ritz-Carlton that day was a disconcerting and freakish coincidence.

At 10:05 A.M., the world stifled a collective cry as the south tower of the World Trade Center, once the mightiest building on earth, seemingly evaporated behind a shroud of dust and smoke. For all the confusion and cloudiness, it was impossible to tell what had happened from television. But for those on the ground, the unthinkable was the only explanation: the tower had collapsed. Twenty minutes later, the north tower met the same fate as its twin, pounding mercilessly into the streets of downtown Manhattan, leaving thousands dead and hundreds more fleeing for their lives.

By noon, New Yorkers were paralyzed in fear, uncertain whether the attacks had ended and unclear as to the safest place to be. By mid-afternoon, all traffic on the island of Manhattan had ceased. Citizens wandered the streets, dialing and redialing their cell phones to contact loved ones, vaguely moving in the direction of their homes. Survivors walked aimlessly northward from what would come to be known as Ground Zero, caked in soot and dust, battered and bleeding, clutching strangers and sobbing. Throngs of shell-shocked Brooklynites marched silently across the Brooklyn Bridge, eager to get home and assure their families of their safety.

In Washington, a state of emergency was declared by 1:30 P.M. The Pentagon ordered five warships and two aircraft carriers to

various locations throughout the East Coast. The ships were sad-
dled with guided missiles capable of shooting down any aircraft
perceived to be a further threat. President Bush had been whisked
from Florida to Louisiana to Nebraska. Colin Powell was on his
way back from Latin America. Donald Rumsfeld was in the Pentagon. By 4:30 P.M., the president was on his way back to Washington, and the first reports of Osama bin Laden's involvement in the
attacks has already been aired. Newspapers would later report that
the bin Laden family members that were in the United States at
the time, of which there were many, were quickly moved to safe locations awaiting their expedited travel arrangements back home
to Saudi Arabia.

During sunset, buildings burned and lurched, cleaved and collapsed, and filled the sky with smoke and dust. Brooklyn, a mile
southeast of Manhattan, lay covered in noxious dust, singed documents, Daytimer pages. The stench of burning plastic perme-
ated every crevice of New York, a stinging reminder of the
already unforgettable events of the day.

At 8:30 P.M., the president, now back at the White House, addressed the nation on television. He spoke of the "thousands of
lives suddenly ended by evil." He boldly claimed that "these acts
shattered steel, but they cannot dent the steel of American re-
solve." And he cast the net of America's vengeance far and wide
in making no distinction between the terrorists who committed
the acts, and those who harbor them.

It is impossible to say whether during the darkest day in
America's history, it dawned on the partners at the Carlyle
Group that what was to come, as a direct result of this attack,
would serve their financial interests. Perhaps it was that very
day, in the midst of the chaos and grief that had gripped the nation. It might have been after they had ascertained the where-
abouts of their many friends at the Pentagon, and the future
started to become clear. Or maybe it was the next day, when
President Bush characterized the attacks in no uncertain terms

as "acts of war." Regardless, there was little doubt by the third day after the attacks that Carlyle was in for some heady times. Congress overwhelmingly approved $40 billion in emergency funds, about half of which was earmarked for the armed services. Also in the works was a massive increase in the Pentagon budget, $33 billion, in time for the Department of Defense's 2002 fiscal year, beginning October 1, 2001.

Cashing in on Tragedy

The partners of Carlyle—Rubenstein, Carlucci, Conway, and D'Aniello—stood to gain the most of anyone in the company, possibly in the country. Those four would have to shake off the devastation of September 11, and look forward to their big payday. It is not an exaggeration to say that September 11 was going to make all of them very, very rich men. This is the reality of the business they chose. And in the defense industry, war time is boom time.

"Capitol Hill is prepared to do whatever the Pentagon wants," said Gordon Adams, a budget official in the Clinton administration, in a *New York Times* piece a week after the attacks. Indeed Capitol Hill provided enough money to the Pentagon to make the budget woes and tough decisions of the past year suddenly irrelevant. Among the weapons programs that had been given new life was, of course, the unkillable gun: the Crusader.

The money was pouring in now and there was no longer any reason to deny the army its precious gun. After the attacks, opponents to the gun were silenced, not wanting to assume the political liabilities of killing a weapons program in the midst of war. On September 26, just two weeks after that attacks, the army signed a $665 million contract with United Defense for the next phase of the Crudader's development. The money would carry the gun maker through 2003. But the first prototype for Crusader was not due to be delivered until 2004, and production of the units would not come for years after. It was highly unlikely the war in Afghanistan would still be ongoing by that time. And nothing had changed the original argument against the gun: it was still too heavy, even at 42 tons, and the need for this type of open battlefield weapon was waning, as the fighting in the caves and tunnels of Afghanistan was demonstrating. But none of that was important anymore. There was enough money to go around for everyone. "A rising tide does lift all boats," said John Williams of the National Defense Industrial Association, in a *New York Times* article.

The defense landscape had changed so dramatically, and so thoroughly, after September 11 that Carlyle quickly and wisely decided it was time to take United Defense public weeks after the attacks on the America. On October 22, 2001, the company filed an S-1 registration with the Securities and Exchange Commission, planning an initial public offering before the end of the year. In the filing, United Defense listed the following as its reasons for selling shares to the public:

1. The U.S. defense budget submission for fiscal 2002 reflects an 11 percent increase over fiscal 2001.
2. Defense procurement and development accounts are growing proportionately with overall national security spending and are expected to continue growing in the near future.
3. The Bush administration's recently published Quadrennial Defense Review calls for retaining the current force structure and increasing investment in next-generation technologies and capabilities to enable U.S. military forces to more effectively counter emerging threats.
4. The terrorist attacks of September 11, 2001, have generated strong congressional support for increased defense spending.

William Conway would later go on the record as saying "No one wants to be a beneficiary of September 11," in a report in *The Nation* entitled "Crony Capitalism Goes Global." Nevertheless, Carlyle took United Defense public on December 14, the day after Congress passed the defense authorization bill allowing for full funding of Crusader program going forward. On that single day, Carlyle took profits of $237 million. On paper, the company had made three times that amount. All the time spent lobbying government officials, calling on old friends, and greasing the palms of congressmen had finally paid off. Crusader was alive and well.

Bin Laden's Business

In the mean time, Carlyle was dealing with yet another public relations crisis, and this one dwarfed all that came before it. Carlyle had been doing business with dozens of families and businesses throughout the Middle East since the early 1990s. And they had been extremely successful in the region. So successful that they had garnered a reputation for having a tremendous amount of influence over the deal flow in the area. After all, the company had been running the Saudi Economic Offset Program for years, a government funded program designed to encourage foreign investment into Saudi Arabia, under the condition that a portion of the profits be reinvested in Saudi Arabia. In a sense, Carlyle had become the gatekeeper to foreign investing in Saudi Arabia.

Not many people knew any of this at the time of the September 11 attacks. But by the end of September, the general public would know far more about Carlyle's business than anyone at Carlyle was comfortable with. In the weeks following the attacks, the name Osama bin Laden leaped onto the forefront of America's consciousness as public enemy number one. Storefronts hung pictures of his likeness, cut out of newspapers, with head-lines of "Wanted: Dead or Alive." Not since the Red Scare of the 1950s had the United States had a more tangible opposition. It seemed that the entire nation was united in its hatred of one man. Then, on September 27, the *Wall Street Journal* ran a story entitled "Bin Laden Family Is Tied to U.S. Group." That group, of course, was Carlyle.

Carlyle had a relationship with the bin Ladens that began in the early 1990s, when they tried to put together a deal for the Italian Petroleum (IP) company. At the time, Basil Al Rahim, a young Carlyle associate, was traveling from Saudi Arabia to Amman to Bahrain, to United Arab Emirates, drumming up support for Carlyle's forthcoming international funds. "I met with 101 different potential clients in 16 days," recalls Al Rahim. "No one had really ever heard of us." Since that time, Carlyle's business in the Middle East blossomed. One of the clients that Al Rahim helped secure was the bin Laden family, which owned a $5 billion construction business by the name of Saudi Binladin Group.

The bin Laden family consists of more than 50 brothers and sisters, all the progeny of Mohammed bin Laden. Osama had his Saudi citizenship revoked in 1991, and was reportedly cut off from his family. Since his father's passing, Bakr bin Laden became the head of the business and the family, and as such he committed money to Carlyle on several occasions. It was a fruit-ful relationship for both parties involved. But now, all of that had changed.

The article in the *Wall Street Journal* pointed out the most stun-ning and atrocious irony of Carlyle's history: through Carlyle, the bin Laden family was in a position to make millions from the war being waged against their own brother. The news that George Bush Sr., James Baker III, and Frank Carlucci had visited the bin Ladens in recent years also stunned the American public. It was, in fact, the Carlyle Partners II fund in which the bin Laden family was invested. The same fund that held United Defense, as well as a host of other defense holdings.

Carlyle told the press that the bin Ladens were only in for $2 million, a relatively small amount of money considering the whole fund was worth $1.3 billion. But one bin Laden family financial representative says the number was much larger. And Al Rahim says that earlier in his time with Carlyle, which ended in 1997, the bin Laden family had several times that amount invested in the company. Regardless of the actual amount, the irony ultimately proved too much for Carlyle, and by the end of October, they severed ties to the family, liquidating their holdings.

A month had elapsed between when the news of Carlyle's bin Laden connection emerged and the company divested their millions. During that time, every major news outlet had picked up the story. Carlyle was sustaining significant collateral damage and was ill-equipped to handle it. Up to this point, Rubenstein had always acted as the company's spokesperson to the press. But this was too much. Calls were pouring in from around the world. Everyone wanted to know about the company that connected the Bush's and the bin Ladens. It was a disaster.

A Congresswoman's Accusations

The company hired a public relations specialist for the first time in its history, but he was overmatched. The press was digging faster and deeper than ever before, dredging up all of the old controversies and conflicts of interest. From sources of varying credibility came claims the now all too familiar charges of cronyism, influence peddling, and dirty dealing in the Middle East. It was all the same accusations the press had levied before, just in greater volume than ever. But it wasn't until an actual elected official called out Carlyle by name that the company started fighting back.

In a March 2002 interview with a Berkeley, California, radio station, Representative Cynthia McKinney, a Democrat from Georgia, spoke publicly what was already making so many Americans uneasy: "Persons close to this administration are poised to make huge profits off America's new war." She went on to say, "An administration of questionable legitimacy has been given unprecedented power . . . We know there were numerous warnings of the events to come on September 11 . . . What did this administration know and when did it know it . . . Who else knew, and why did they not warn the innocent people of New York who were needlessly murdered . . . What do they have to hide?"

In the address, McKinney named the Carlyle Group as an example of the cronyism she was talking about. McKinney was implying that the Bush administration knew the attacks were coming, allowed them to happen, and was now reaping the profits, both financial and political, through its connections to the Carlyle Group. The comments resonated with a growing group of cynics on the Internet and spread like wildfire across the Web. For weeks there had been reports of an intelligence breakdown and foreknowledge of the attacks in the major news outlets. McKinney was simply giving a voice to what many already suspected. And she was absolutely lambasted for it.

Carlyle spokesman Chris Ullman, in easily his most entertaining, not to mention effective, public statement in his six months on the job asked the press if McKinney had "said these things while standing on a grassy knoll in Roswell, New Mexico?" And the public lashing was on. Representative Johnny Isakson, a Republican from Georgia, said McKinney has "demonstrated in Washington a total lack of responsibility in her statements." Senator Zell Miller from Georgia called her "very dangerous and irresponsible." Kathleen Parker, a nationally syndicated columnist, called McKinney's statements "idiotic" and bordering on treason. Parker suggested the advent of a new award, the McKinney Award, "for people too stupid to serve in public office."

Parker also pointed out that it was McKinney that publicly admonished New York Mayor Rudolph Giuliani for declining Prince Alwaleed's offer of $10 million in aid after the September 11 attacks. McKinney offered to find appropriate charities for the Prince's money if he still wanted to donate it. He didn't.

McKinney would eventually back off a little from her comments, issuing a statement saying "I am not aware of any evidence showing that President Bush or members of his administration have personally profited from the attacks of 9/11. A complete investigation might reveal that to be the case." In the end, McKinney received vindication when it became clear that a complete investigation would indeed be necessary, as enough information had emerged that indicated Bush's prior knowledge of the attacks. But McKinney's over-the-top comments probably did more damage than good in the drive to address the truly important issues surrounding the Carlyle Group. Charles Lewis, executive director of the Center for Public Integrity, said the comments undermined the important work the center has been trying to complete in regards to Carlyle by making a "caricature of the issues that may make it easily dismissible."

McKinney was certainly an easy target to discredit. And by August her previously loyal constituents voted her out of office. But at least part of what she said in that interview was dead on: Persons close to the Bush administration were in fact in a position to gain financially from the September 11 attacks, as the United Defense IPO had already demonstrated. But there were other ways the company was getting rich off the events of that day as well. Lots of ways. And September 11 was turning into an outright bonanza for the boys at Carlyle.

Beyond Big Guns

Most of the American public first heard of anthrax a week after the attacks on the World Trade Center, when a granular substance was found in letters sent to NBC news in New York and the *New York Post* offices. But the deadly virus soon found a permanent place in the American terrorist lexicon when every day brought new cases of infection. First it was an editorial assistant at the *Post* who noticed a blister on her finger: cutaneous anthrax. Then an assistant to NBC anchor Tom Brokaw found a lesion. Then a photo editor at *The Sun* in Boca Raton. Mail sorting facilities were shut down. News media outlets were on edge, and stopped opening their mail. In many ways, the anthrax scare had Americans more on edge than the September 11 attacks. It seemed more insidious, like we were seeing the beginnings of what could ultimately be a far more deadly act of terror.

And the terror spread rapidly, from mail processing facilities in Trenton, New Jersey, to the Hart Senate Office building in Washington, DC. The country was ill-equipped to handle this kind of an attack, psychologically or logistically. Building after building was shut down, crippling postal service and severely inhibiting the Beltway's political machine. The government gave mixed messages on a daily basis, encouraging citizens not to panic, while at the same time warning of the lethality of anthrax. It was a confusing, fearful time for the whole country. But once again, Carlyle had the uncanny ability to be at the right place at the right time, and profit from the situation.

Carlyle owned 25 percent of a Pittsburgh, Pennsylvania–based company called IT Group, an environmental and hazardous waste cleanup specialist. At the time of the anthrax attacks, IT Group was in bad shape, suffering under the weight of nearly $700 million worth of debt, and on the verge of declaring bankruptcy.

In the wake of the anthrax attacks, IT Group scored a number of cleanup contracts with anthrax-infected buildings. Among the new work coming their way was the contract for the Hart Senate Office Building and the Trenton postal facility. The company had 400 workers on site at various locations working 24 hours a day, 7 days a week to clean up anthrax spores. It was snapping up contracts with government agencies left and right, like the General

Services Administration, the Army Corp of Engineers, the Center for Disease Control and Prevention, and the U.S. Navy. Richard Conte, vice president and treasurer of IT Group would tell reporters that the anthrax work "is very good for our bottom line." For a moment, it looked as if IT Group was going to miraculously save itself from bankruptcy and emerge one of the few winners in the war on terrorism.

But the anthrax scare turned out to be much more limited an attack than was originally feared. In the end, IT Group still declared bankruptcy and was bought out by the Shaw Group for $105 million plus close to $95 million in assumed debt, a price that presumably would have been much lower had anthrax never burst on the scene and given IT Group some last minute business. Carlyle had saved at least some of its bacon.

Then rumors spread around the Internet that Carlyle was also invested in a company called Bioport, which held the only government contract on an experimental and highly controversial anthrax vaccine. The company has retired Admiral William Crowe, a man who was chairman of the Joint Chiefs of Staff while Carlucci was secretary of defense. The two know each other well, but Carlyle's involvement with the company is unknown. Both companies are private, and as such have no obligation to disclose investments to the public. Carlyle Group spokesperson Chris Ullman asserts that Carlyle has nothing to do with Bioport.

There were other ways that Carlyle was capitalizing on both the airplane attacks and the anthrax letters: security. Deep in the belly of a mountain in Boyers, Pennsylvania, exists an underground facility carved into rock that holds one of Carlyle's most important investments, U.S. Investigations Services. USIS, as it is known, is a classic example of privatization, and a classic Carlyle investment. Once known as the U.S. Civil Service Commission, then the U.S. Office of Personnel Management (OPM), and finally the Office of Federal Investigations (OFI), the organization was a staple of the U.S. government's ability to gather information on any individual applying for a job with the government. Its charter, as it had been from the beginning, was to investigate the backgrounds of government employees, and provide them with varying levels of national security clearance. USIS's cave-like work environment is something that only James Bond could love. Rock walls, tight security, no open-toed shoes, and no open flames—employees have steamed lunches brought into the facility every day. The former mine is also home to the personnel files of thousands of government officials. It is top secret stuff.

The company's history, like most of the companies in Carlyle Partners II, is highly controversial. Since going private in 1996, USIS has been incredibly successful. But getting private wasn't so easy. Employees of the government-run Office of Federal Investigations fought the privatization the whole way, fearing layoffs and salary cuts. They hired lawyers, testified at congressional hearings, and protested the decision to take it private, which was made by the Clinton administration. To quiet them down, the government offered the investigators an employee stock ownership plan (ESOP) and promised them the same or better salaries in the newly formed private enterprise. After years of acrimonious battles, the Office of Federal Investigations became USIS in July 1996. Employees retired from OFI and started work the next day at USIS.

As life under the ESOP went on, some employees felt they had been duped. One former USIS employee says that USIS executives harassed older investigators, encouraging them to leave the company so they could hire younger employees, who wouldn't vest in the stock plan for five years. That left more of the equity pie to the high-level executives, should the company ever go public or sell itself. Before USIS had gone private though, the only investigators allowed to work on national security investigations had to have five years experience. That meant that the company would have to rely on less experienced investigators for some of the most important jobs in the country. Many of the older investigators then left in disgust. The result was a watering down of the talent at USIS, and many blamed Carlyle for the changes.

The company was growing profits and acquiring smaller firms by the turn of the century. But nothing would compare to the explosion of business after September 11. "Since 9/11, USIS's acquisition of contracts has exploded," said one employee that declined to be identified. "All the new FAA, Department of Transportation, Transportation Security Administration, INS, Customs, . . . all of those employees being hired are being investigated by USIS. They also have contracts with all the major airlines, and the contract companies who provide airport security. I do not exaggerate when I say that Carlyle is taking over the world in government contract work, particularly defense work. Carlyle is a one-world shadow government."

USIS is just one more example of how Carlyle was in a frighteningly good position to reap the benefits of September 11. There are more examples, like EG&G, a company Carlyle bought in the summer of 1999, which makes, among other things, the X-ray scanners that are used in airports. Whether the company is a "shadow government," is for conspiracy theorists to debate. But the company's uncanny ability to be in the right place at the right time sure doesn't help to dissuade the cynics.

Crusader Denouement

By 2002, Carlyle's decade of cultivating ties with prominent politicians and acquiring countless defense contractors was really paying off. President Bush was creating an Office of Homeland Security, and Secretary of Defense Rumsfeld was talking of the war on terrorism being a long, drawn out affair, perhaps something that never ends. Defense budgets were soaring and

Carlyle was already looking to take other defense-related businesses public in the coming year.

After the unrelenting bad press about the Crusader approval reached a fever pitch in Washington, Rumsfeld, at the behest of Deputy Secretary of Defense Paul Wolfowitz, finally gave the order to kill the gun once and for all, but only after United Defense had already made gobs of money from its public offering. It also came after Rumsfeld was publicly embarrassed by an Army-sponsored lobbying campaign of Congress that went on behind Rumsfeld's back, after the Defense Secretary had already made it clear the program was to be cancelled. The actions on the part of the Army would result in Rumsfeld launching an investigation (still ongoing) and excoriating those responsible for the clandestine lobbying effort. "I have a minimum of high regard for that kind of behavior," Rumsfeld would tell the press in an article by the Associated Press.

But Carlyle had already taken its profits. And besides, the very same day the U.S. Army officially notified United Defense of the termination of the Crusader contract, that same Army awarded United Defense a brand new contract for a new artillery system, much like the Crusader only much, much lighter.

"United Defense and its industry partners welcome the new contract and the challenge of bringing the technological advances matured in the Crusader program to the Objective Force and the Future Combat System," said Keith Howe, vice president and general manager of United Defense's Armament Systems Division, in the same press release that announced the end of the Crusader contract. "The contract recognizes the tremendous capability and the performance of the over 2,200 employees nationwide that brought Crusader to the Army's Proving Ground and who will now focus their energies and talents on the need to field a less than 20-ton system to the Army by 2008."

Everyone was happy with the result. Rumsfeld and Carlyle avoided a damaging public relations fiasco over the Crusader by killing the program in a decidedly public manner. The Army was assured of getting an even better gun in the same time frame as the Crusader had been promised. And United Defense got to prop up its stock price by announcing the new contract the day they announced the death of the old contract, without ever skipping a beat. It was classic Carlyle. United Defense also picked up in September 2002, a contract to provide Taiwan with $250 million worth of amphibious assault vehicles. The deal happened after Carlucci, who is the chairman of the U.S.–Taiwan Business Council, met with Tang Yao-Ming, the defense minister in Taiwan. Just another day in Carlyle's global playground.

The saga of Crusader is one of the clearest examples of how Carlyle does business. To the outside observer, the company lives on the edge, deftly maneuvering its way through the revolving door of politics and business. Keenly aware of public opinion, and how to manage the press, Carlyle has always been able to avoid the kind of scandal that brings a company down. "No one has any proof because there is no proof," explains Chris Ullman, the company's spokesperson.

Though more financial companies are learning from Carlyle's example—hiring politicians like Al Gore or Rudolph Giuliani, during their political downtime—we may never see another company like Carlyle. The sheer volume of political capital the company has amassed in its 15 years of existence is unprecedented, and would be nearly impossible to duplicate.

With $13 billion under management, close to 500 employees throughout the world, and hundreds of defense, aerospace, telecom and health care companies in their portfolio, it is safe to say that Carlyle has already gone well beyond Eisenhower's vision of a military industrial complex. There is every indication that with the current administration, and war remaining on the foreseeable horizon, Carlyle's power and reach may exceed anything Eisenhower might have imagined when he first warned against the formation of an Iron Triangle.

The important thing to remember is that the story of Carlyle, while it makes good reading, is still young. The amount of influence the company wields is already disconcerting, but at only 15 years old, the company is in a relative infancy. The potential of the company should not be underestimated, and a healthy dose of paranoia is probably in order when viewing any of the Carlyle Group's actions. As America's most revered companies are brought down through scandals and abuses of the public's trust, it has never been more important for the average citizen to remain vigilant and skeptical, of our country's business and political leaders, even during war time, when we are expected to be exceedingly patriotic. While the Carlyle Group is certainly not about patriotism, it is a uniquely American story. It is about money, power, war, and politics. All of the things that build America's might, and compromise its integrity.

EPILOGUE

It may well be that writing a book about the Carlyle Group in 2003 is a premature exercise. The company is, after all, only 15 years old, and is just now hitting its stride. In fact, the future holds even more intrigue for this private equity behemoth than the past.

In the summer of 2002, Carlyle helped form the China Venture Capital Association, a nebulous organization charged with warding off corruption in China and strengthening ties with the Chinese government. Chang Sun, the chairman of the group, said "within the industry we need to have a minimal level of code of conduct so that we don't have people who ruin the reputation of the industry. We will talk about how to regulate ourselves rather than be regulated by the government." A truly scary prospect, but nothing we haven't seen before.

China, like Saudi Arabia decades ago, is fertile ground for American investment. Edging its way toward a more capitalistic society, China is still a massive untapped market controlled largely by the government: a combination tailor made for Carlyle's special brand of access capitalism. In other words, watch this space.

Another area to keep an eye on would be Europe. In the fall of 2002, Carlyle completed an acquisition of Qinetiq, the research and development arm of the United Kingdom's Ministry of

Defense. When news of the acquisition broke in England, the MOD came under fire for potentially compromising the national security of the United Kingdom by selling such a crucial unit to an American company run by so many ex-politicians. Fiona Draper, a representative of the trade union Prospect, which includes the scientists at Qinetiq, told reporters, "the fact that they are a foreign company will obviously exacerbate my members concerns, given Carlyle's fairly opaque structure, there must be concerns over whether undue influence may be brought to bear which may not be in Britain's interest."

The "opaque structure" to which Draper refers is not uncommon for private companies, especially private equity companies. The nature of the business is such that a private company buys other private companies, none of which are obligated to reveal their financial records. All of which makes gathering information on Carlyle very challenging. Though it excels in buying and selling businesses that are under heavy government regulation, Carlyle itself is under almost no scrutiny from federal overseers. The only thing keeping Carlyle the least bit honest at this point is public interest groups and the media. And at a time when American patriotism is at an all-time high following the attacks on the World Trade Center and the Pentagon, criticizing the current president and his father for questionable business practices is a tricky business. There is frighteningly little tolerance for muckraking at the moment.

When Carlyle was notified of this book, the company immediately circled its wagons, declining to allow any interviews of its employees and waging what one insider termed as a "scorched earth campaign," instructing anyone that could be used as a source to clam up. Several people who have spoken to the partners about this book said the company is "scared to death" of the publicity that is sure to follow.

It is common for former employees of the company to fear that Carlyle will somehow discern their identities if they speak to reporters, either on or off the record, and ruin them. The company has required many of its ex-employees to sign nondisclosure agreements, or gag orders, instructing them not to talk about their work to the press, a highly unusual move. The result of the company essentially pleading the fifth is that they maintain plausible deniability of anything written about them. But the unintended effect is that it makes them appear as if they have something damaging to hide. All the while, Carlyle executives take umbrage at the mere suggestion that the company is secretive. Yet the names of some of their most prominent employees, like George H. W. Bush, is not listed anywhere on the company's Web site. There are many things this company doesn't want anyone to know.

Conspiracy theorists that obsess on secret societies and outlandish plots overlook the more insidious and destructive effects of a company like Carlyle. By insinuating itself into the very fabric of the world's economic structure, Carlyle has accomplished far more than any Trilateral Commission or Masonic society could dream. They have made themselves an indispensable part of the international community's cash flow. Millions of people are invested in Carlyle and don't even know it, like the 1.3 million people relying on CalPERS to manage their pension fund. Do they even know that CalPERS is a part owner of Carlyle?

Ultimately, the success of the Carlyle Group depends on its continuing ability to gain access to high-level government officials, thereby getting a jump on policy changes, both domestic and international. And that access hinges on Carlyle's remarkable track record of hiring the most powerful men in the world. To keep their stockpile of political powerhouses fresh, don't be surprised to see the company reach deep into the current Bush administration after the president leaves office and snare anyone from Colin Powell to Dick Cheney to Donald Rumsfeld to George W. Bush himself. The revolving door to Carlyle is always turning.

Though company officials are outwardly amused by the rumors and accusations that swirl around Carlyle, there is a reason why

people fear them. It's difficult to explain away certain aspects of
the company. Like why George Bush Sr., in the face of mounting
criticism and the undermining of his son's credibility in office,
doesn't simply resign from the company? He is already wealthy,
with his family's legacy secure. And there must be a thousand different job opportunities available for the ex-president that don't
involve obvious conflicts of interest or incidents of international
political intrigue. Or why James Baker III, with his own law firm
and a foundation that bears his name, feels the need to continue
toiling for a firm that clearly threatens his heretofore untarnished
reputation? It begs the question: What are these men up to?

From Watergate to Iran-Contra to Lewinsky-gate, the public
and the press have performed admirably in keeping our politicians honest, or at least accountable, while they are in office. But
the civil checks and balances mechanism breaks down after politicians leave office. The power and influence of politicians dimin-
ishes upon their retirement from public service, but it is still
formidable. And the work that Carlyle's ex-politicos perform, both
in nature and in scale, is unlike anything that's come before them.
That's why Carlyle will continue to be both a compelling story to
follow, as well as a cautionary tale.

AFTERWORD

In a move that *BusinessWeek* immediately characterized as an attempt to "scramble the conspiracy theories," Carlyle named Lou Gerstner, the long time IBM Chairman and CEO, as Frank Carlucci's successor to the chairman position at Carlyle. Carlucci retained the role of "Chairman Emeritus." Charles Lewis of the Center for Public Integrity was quoted in the *New York Times* as saying, "I'm not sure what the motive is, but this does seem to be a move away from Carlyle's image of cashing in on the old Washington rolodex."

Gerstner will certainly bring a new sense of financial credibility to Carlyle, on which he plans to spend about 20 percent of his time, according to the Carlyle press release. It will certainly be a significant bolstering of the business side of the Iron Triangle. At IBM, Gerstner led a stunning reversal of the computer maker's fortunes through the 1990s and, unlike many tech CEOs of late, leaves with his company and his legacy well intact. His knowledge of global markets will be invaluable to Carlyle.

But the company will still be run by Rubenstein, Conway, and D'Aniello, just like it always has been. And newcomers to Carlyle should not be fooled by the impeccable pedigree of Gerstner: This is still a company that made its fortunes on the strength of political power. And it is likely that it always will be.

Appendix A

COMPANY CAPSULES

Carlyle is among the largest private equity firms in the world. It employs 491 people in 21 worldwide offices. It has more than 535 investors from more than 55 different countries. And as of June 2002, the company had over $13.5 billion under management in 21 different funds. Following is a small sampling of the hundreds of companies that have been a part of the Carlyle family since the firm's founding in 1987. From the list, which is merely the tip of the iceberg, it is clear how thoroughly Carlyle has insinuated itself into the political, military, and financial fabric of the United States. From security to weapons to information technology, Carlyle has all of the bases covered.

United Defense was born from a partnership between Harsco and FMC, or Food Machinery Corp., when the two combined their defense units in 1994. The company made a name for itself by producing the Bradley Fighting Vehicles, which was used to great effect during Desert Storm. The company was bought by Carlyle in 1997, in the midst of a major political battle over the future of its next-generation fighting vehicle, a massive mobile howitzer called Crusader. After a contentious battle to save the gun program, despite widespread opposition, the Crusader program was cancelled in the summer of 2002, after United Defense had gone public in December 2001. United Defense was subsequently awarded another contract for the development of a new next-generation gun for the Army. Carlyle remains the majority shareholder.

USIS was originally a government-run agency called the Office of Federal Investigations. U.S. Investigations Services is a private company, headquartered in an underground bunker facility in western Pennsylvania, that performs background checks on virtually all government employees, airline employees, and preemployment checks for corporate hires. The company has more than 3,600 employees, most of which are investigators, and operates in 178 locations throughout the United States. It performs more than one million cases a year for the federal government. Carlyle invested in USIS as a strategic partner in October 1999.

Vinnell is one of the oldest companies to make an appearance in Carlyle's portfolio. Vinnell has a long, but mysterious past. Originally a heavy construction company that built airstrips in Vietnam, Vinnell burst onto the forefront of the public's consciousness when in 1975 the company signed a multimillion dollar contract with the Saudi Arabian royal family, agreeing to train the Saudi National Guard, a private army charged with protecting the Saudi monarchy. The company pioneered a wave of military privatization, leading the way for dozens of similar mercenary outfits. The company claims to have operated on behalf of the U.S. government in more than 50 countries on five continents. But recent revelations have indicated that the company, at least at one time, served as a cover for CIA activity in the Middle East. Vinnell was bought by BDM, a Carlyle company, in 1992. It was then purchased by TRW in 1997.

BDM is historically one of the most successful defense consultants in history. Thanks to its erstwhile CEO Earle Williams, the company became a player in the defense contracting business in Washington during the 1980s, and was bought by the Carlyle Group in 1990 from Loral, which had acquired the company from Ford Aerospace. After a rocky past, BDM settled in under Carlyle, doing more business in the burgeoning Saudi Arabian market. BDM was among the few companies that stayed on in Saudi Arabia during the Gulf War, a fact that was not lost on the royal family, or Saudi citizens, who bombed the office buildings of BDM in 1994.

Composite Structures is a maker of composite and metal-bond structures. Its products can be found on everything from fighter jets to Apache helicopters to missiles. The company does about $60 million in annual sales and employs 350 people. Among the military aircraft products that Composite manufactures are: AH-64 Apache Helicopter; C-17 Military Transport Jet; and the Bell UH-1 Military Helicopter Series. The Carlyle Group is a part owner of Composite Structures, which it purchased from Alcoa in the late 1990s.

EG&G is named after its 1931 co-founding triumvirate, Harold Edgerton, Kenneth Germeshausen, and Herbert Grier. EG&G has been involved in everything from the Manhattan Project to modern day weapons design and analysis. Among the company's clients are the Departments of Energy, Defense, Treasury, and Transportation. It's annual sales are estimated at $500 million, and it employs more than 4,500 people. Carlyle bought the company outright in August 1999.

Federal Data Corporation is the premier provider of information technology services to the U.S. government. Federal Data Corporation boasts contracts with everyone from the Air Force to the Internal Revenue Service, and lots in between. Its annual revenues exceed $500 million, and it has more that 1,400 employees. Carlyle bought the company in 1995 for under $100 million, and grew its revenues in 5 years from $140 million to $538 million, then sold the company to Northrop Grumman in 2000 for $302 million.

Lier Siegler Services Inc. (LSI) is a major military contractor, providing logistics support, or supply and maintenance, of a variety of military aircraft programs. LSI has managed the Royal Saudi Air Force Peace Hawk program for more than 14 years. It provides maintenance and refurbishment for Army vehicles throughout Europe. It contracts with the Air Force for the F-15, F-5, and AH-1 aircrafts. And it has provided Army vehicle maintenance and modification since 1980, including work on the Bradley Fighting Vehicles, a United Defense product. The company was bought by Carlyle in September 1997.

Vought Aircraft is perhaps the company with the longest and richest history in the Carlyle portfolio. Vought has been making military aircraft and missiles since before the first World War. The company has worked on dozens of famous fighters and bombers, including the F-8, B1-B, C-17, and B-2 bombers. Carlyle originally bought a stake in the company in the early 1990s, only to sell it to Northrop Grumman and buy the company back outright in July 2000.

Appendix B

CARLYLE CORRESPONDENCES

UNCLASSIFIED

200103677

THE CARLYLE GROUP
1001 Pennsylvania Avenue, N.W.
Washington, D.C. 20004-2505
(202) 347-2626
(202) 347-1818 (Fax)

CI 区'' -5 配 ..

February 23, 2001

RELEASED IN FULL

The Honorable Colin Powell
U.S. Department of State
2201 C Street, N.W.
Harry S. Truman Building
Washington, DC 20520

Dear Secretary Powell:

We congratulate you on your great start as Secretary of State. We recognize that there is no shortage of serious issues seeking your attention, but one of the earliest will certainly be Montenegro's relationship to Serbia.

As you know, Montenegro is the last of the five original non-Serbian republics to press its claim for independence. President Djukanovic was in Washington recently, and I hosted a long and spirited talk for several of us with Djukanovic to discuss his thinking. Djukanovic is, of course, a proven friend and ally of the United States, whose supportive role during the NATO bombing campaign helped diminish the threat to American and allied airmen. He also took great risks to oppose Milosevic and aid the Serbian democrats during their darkest hours. He protected Mr. Djindjic and many other Serbian democrats during the Kosovo war, and since 1998 has sheltered high rates of Kosovo refugees of all ethnic groups. He has been the engine of pro-Western change in this heretofore-solidly pro-Milosevic society, though he understands that Montenegro has further to go to achieve full democratization and economic reform. Montenegro will for some time remain a divided society whether or not it obtains independence, since Montenegrins who allied themselves with Milosevic continue to side with Belgrade on retaining the FRY.

Djukanovic struck us as determined to proceed to independence. He plans to hold special parliamentary elections April 22, which – if the pro-independence parties gain a majority – he intends to follow up with a referendum on independence 45-to-60 days later. If he obtains over 50 percent of the vote in the referendum, he plans to declare independence and then begin a serious negotiation with Serbia about the future nature of their relations. He said that he views independence as a means to achieve full democracy, market efficiency, and integration with Europe. By taking over the functions of security, foreign affairs, trade, customs, currency, and economic management during Montenegro's tenure as the key U.S. ally in the region, Djukanovic maintains the country has already acquired *de facto* independence.

Djukanovic stressed that he planned to achieve independence democratically and non-violently without destabilizing the region. He expressed confidence that all Montenegrins, despite their political differences, would respect the majority decision in a referendum. He said he understood that the real issue behind the coolness of Washington and the Europeans toward Montenegrin independence was not Montenegro itself but the impact of independence on Kosovo.

Djukanovic said the Kosovo problem had originated long ago and escalated after Milosevic had revoked Kosovo's constitutional autonomy. Then came the massive Serbian military intervention and NATO's war. Meanwhile, Montenegro had maintained good relations with the Albanians, and Djukanovic had established a multiethnic state and cooperated with ethnic Albanian political parties in Montenegro.

UNCLASSIFIED

UNCLASSIFIED

The Honorable Colin Powell
February 23, 2001
Page Two

He said it was inaccurate to claim that Yugoslavia was the only framework for solving the Kosovo problem, as it was not solved when Yugoslavia existed. A solution could only come through the efforts of Belgrade and Pristina with the help of the international community. He underlined that Montenegro was irrelevant to this process and that the success of Montenegro's multiethnic governance and reforms would have a stabilizing impact on both Serbia and Albanian communities in the region.

In his view, Belgrade was just trying to frighten the international community by raising the problems of Kosovo, Macedonia, Greece, and the independence of Bosnia's Republika Srpska. The Bosnia problem, he said, was "nonsense," stressing that Republika Srpska was a problem because of Serb nationalism in Belgrade. "Belgrade tries to scare the international community that Montenegro's independence will cause Republika Srpska's secession, while all the time Belgrade is supporting Republika Srpska," he noted.

He drew our attention to Belgrade media reporting that the U.S. by refusing to receive him at your level had rejected Montenegro's independence effort. Despite this, the Serbs were still generally anti-American, while the Montenegrins were pro-American. Serbia had refused to cooperate with the Hague tribunal, while Djukanovic indicated that he would arrest indictees residing in Montenegro if the chief prosecutor handed him any sealed indictments.

Asked whether he thought that maintaining the FRY would promote stability or instability, he said there was no question that it would be destabilizing: "So long as Yugoslavia exists, Serbian nationalism lives on. The concept of Greater Serbia is not gone."

He said much of Europe was unhelpfully inclined toward the status quo. Despite the fact that Montenegro had met the terms of the European Union's own Badinter Commission on independence for the Yugoslav republics, most Europeans had gone back on these principles, especially the two nations most friendly to Belgrade, France and Italy. These legal and performance principles were the same ones by which the EU and U.S. had recognized Slovenia's independence, which is now favored by many for NATO membership.

At the conclusion of the meeting, he asked that the U.S. return to the position that, while you prefer Montenegro to remain part of the FRY, if the process to independence is open and democratic, the U.S. would accept it. On behalf of Mort Abramowitz, Max Kampelman, Jeane Kirkpatrick, Richard Perle, Steve Solarz, and Hal Sonnenfeldt, we believe this position makes good policy sense and would be prepared to discuss it with you.

Best wishes,

Frank C. Carlucci
Chairman

UNCLASSIFIED

UNCLASSIFIED

3/14

S/S #200103677

United States Department of State

Washington, D.C. 20520

ACTION MEMORANDUM
S/S

'01 ... 14 ...

CLP

UNCLASSIFIED

RELEASED IN FULL

TO: The Secretary

FROM: EUR - James F. Dobbins

SUBJECT: Response to Letter from Frank Carlucci

203
3/19

Issue for Decision

• Whether to sign attached response to Frank Carlucci, who has written you regarding the Administration's policy towards Montenegro.

Mr. Carlucci wrote to you on February 23 regarding the Administration's policy towards the Government of Montenegro, asking that you take a more forthcoming position on the issue of independence. He writes also on behalf of Mort Abramowitz, Max Kampelman, Jeanne Kirkpatrick, Richard Perle, Steve Solarz and Hal Sonnenfeldt. At the end of the letter, he offers a meeting to discuss this issue further.

While there is no harm in such a meeting, I am not sure that it would be worth your time. The discussion at such a meeting would likely go beyond Montenegro. Attached are two alternate replies. The first does not pick up the offer of a meeting, the second does.

Recommendation(s)

That you sign the attached letter to Mr. Carlucci, which does not offer a meeting.

Approve **CLP** _____ Disapprove_____

Alternatively, that you sign the attached letter to Mr. Carlucci, agreeing to a meeting to discuss Montenegro.

Approve_____   Disapprove_____

Attachments:
   Tab 1 - Proposed reply which does not offer a meeting.
   Tab 2   Proposed reply offering a meeting.
   Tab 3 - Letter from Mr. Carlucci.

UNCLASSIFIED

UNITED STATES DEPARTMENT OF STATE
REVIEW AUTHORITY: DONALD A. JOHNSTON
DATE/CASE ID: 29 APR 2002 200104059

UNCLASSIFIED

THE CARLYLE GROUP
1001 Pennsylvania Avenue, N.W.
Washington, D.C. 20004-2505
(202) 347-2626
(202) 347-1818 (Fax)

February 15, 2001

Granted

Secretary Donald H. Rumsfeld
Department of Defense
Rm. 3E880
1000 Defense Pentagon
Washington, D.C. 20301-1000

Dear Don,

Thanks for the lunch last Friday. It was great seeing you in such good spirits even if you are "all alone."

We thought it useful to follow up on our discussions on the need for reductions in the infrastructure of the Department – and how that might best be done. Over the past three years, the two of us have served as senior advisors to the BENS Tail-to-Tooth Commission. We believe the Commission has addressed the most critical areas that must be tackled if we are to cut the cost of defense infrastructure and re-invest the savings in modernization and other priority programs.

Because the "what to do" is so well known, the beauty of the Commission's report is not in the issues it identifies – rather, it is the focus on implementation, the "how to do it," that sets it apart.

We have taken the liberty of enclosing copies of this package and would be happy to discuss it with you or your staff. Or, perhaps more helpful, we would be pleased to introduce to you, or to whomever you might designate, the Commissioners who put this effort together.

Best regards,

Sincerely,   Sincerely,

Frank C. Carlucci   William J. Perry

THE SECRETARY OF DEFENSE
WASHINGTON

APR 3 2001

Honorable Frank C. Carlucci
Honorable William J. Perry
The Carlyle Group
1001 Pennsylvania Avenue, NW
Washington, DC 20004

Granted

Dear Frank and Bill:

     My apologies for the delay in getting back to you on your letter of February 15th

     There is no question but that we are going to have to tackle the infrastructure issue. I've been impressed with the BENS Tail-to-Tooth Commission report, and congratulate you folks for good work. What I may do is ask the two of you come in and meet with some of the key staff folks who are working on those types of things here in the department.

     I will be back in touch with you. With my appreciation and best wishes,

                      Sincerely,

U06812 /01

State of Connecticut
Office of the Treasurer

DENISE L. NAPPIER
TREASURER

HOWARD G. RIFKIN
DEPUTY TREASURER

September 30, 1999

David M. Rubenstein
Carlyle Asia Partners, L.P.
1001 Pennsylvania Avenue, N.W.
Suite 220 South
Washington, D.C. 20004-2505

Dear Mr. Rubenstein:

As part of an ongoing federal investigation, the United States Attorney for the District of Connecticut recently disclosed a series of improper and illegal activities engaged in by my predecessor, Paul J. Silvester.

The information detailed by the United States Attorney focused, in part, on improper use of finder's fees. While it is my understanding that use of such fees can, in certain circumstances, be a legitimate business practice, the federal investigation has raised a myriad of legal and ethical issues, including possible and probable conflicts of interest and appearances of impropriety. In our effort to comply with the spirit and letter of all Connecticut and federal laws, and consistent with my long-standing interest in public disclosure, it is necessary that we formally ask all firms and individuals doing business with the Office of the State Treasurer to disclose finder's fees or other compensation paid to anyone as a part of any transaction related to the introduction, award, or continuation of business with my Office.

Accordingly, I request that you provide, on the forms enclosed herewith, a detailed disclosure of any and all finder's fees, placement fees, consulting contracts or other compensation currently made in connection with any transaction or ongoing arrangements related to procuring or doing business with the Office of the State Treasurer, as well as any such arrangements during the past five (5) years. As part of this disclosure, I ask that you identify the individuals or entities receiving any such compensation and the amount of each such payment. In the event your company did not pay finder's fees, placement agent fees or furnish other compensation at any time during this period, kindly so indicate in your response. In addition, be advised that such disclosure will continue to be the policy of this administration. For your convenience, these forms may be downloaded from my website, www.state.ct.us/ott/.

Please forward your response on or before October 15, 1999 to the attention of Catherine E. LaMarr, Esq., General Counsel, Office of the State Treasurer, 55 Elm Street, Hartford, Connecticut 06106-1773. Should you have any questions regarding this request, you may contact Christine Shaw, Esq., Chief Executive Assistant, at (860) 702-3211.

My Office values our relationships with each of our vendors and we appreciate your prompt and careful attention to this matter.

Sincerely,

Denise L. Nappier
State Treasurer

55 ELM STREET, HARTFORD, CONNECTICUT 06106-1773, TELEPHONE: (860) 702-3000
AN EQUAL OPPORTUNITY EMPLOYER

State of Connecticut
Office of the Treasurer

DENISE L. NAPPIER
TREASURER

November 5, 1999

David M. Rubenstein
Carlyle European Partners
1001 Pennsylvania Avenue, N.W.
Suite 220 South
Washington, D.C. 20004-2505

Dear Mr. Rubenstein:

By letter dated September 30, 1999, I requested that your company voluntarily disclose all compensation paid or promised in connection with any transaction or ongoing arrangements related to procuring or doing business with the Office of the State Treasurer since January 1, 1995. To date, we have not received a response to this request. In the event you already have submitted your full and complete disclosure, you may disregard this letter.

Disclosure of this information is the policy of this administration. Failure to comply will certainly jeopardize your company's current business relationship with the Office of the State Treasurer, as well as any prospects for future business. Please forward your response on or before November 15, 1999 to the attention of Catherine E. LaMarr, Esq., General Counsel, Office of the State Treasurer, 55 Elm Street, Hartford, Connecticut 06106-1773. Should you have any questions regarding this request, you may contact Christine Shaw, Esq., Chief Executive Assistant, at (860) 702-3211.

In the event we do not receive a full and complete response by the close of business on November 15th, we will work with Connecticut's Attorney General to pursue every legal recourse available to suspend or end our business relationship with your firm.

Sincerely,

Denise L. Nappier
State Treasurer

55 ELM STREET, HARTFORD, CONNECTICUT 06106-1773, TELEPHONE: (860) 702-3000
AN EQUAL OPPORTUNITY EMPLOYER

ACKNOWLEDGMENTS

Researching and reporting this book presented me with a number of unique challenges. First, the Carlyle Group has a very obvious fear of publicity and, as a result, declined to be interviewed for the project. The company went a step further and notified many of their friends, former colleagues, and business partners, if contacted, not to cooperate with the author. Some of them respected the wishes of the folks at Carlyle, some of them did not, and some just fell between the cracks. But with the exception of a brave few, most notably Stephen Norris, almost all of the sources that still had direct contact with Carlyle either declined to be interviewed or would do so only if their identities remained anonymous. There is a very real fear of retribution out there.

All quotations are either from those that said them or from those that overheard the words being spoken, unless otherwise attributed to a newspaper or magazine article. I would like to thank Tim Shorrock for his work with *The Nation,* Michael Lewis for his work in *New Republic,* and Leslie Wayne for her work in the *New York Times.* And I would have been lost without the work of dozens of journalists from the *Washington Post,* which witnessed and chronicled the birth and rise of the Carlyle Group, understanding its impact and import every step of the way. I would also like to thank *Harper's Magazine,* the *Houston Chronicle,* and Jeffrey Toobin, the author of *Too Close To Call: The Thirty-Six Day Battle to Decide the 2000 Election,* from which I gained all of my knowledge of the events that took place in Florida following the 2000 election.

In addition, I would like to thank my editors at Red Herring, particularly Duff McDonald, Blaise Zerega, and Jason Pontin. I would also like to thank my editor at John Wiley & Sons, Jeanne Glasser, for believing in this project.

And most importantly, thank you to my family, friends, and especially my wife Michelle, without whom I would not have been able to complete the task at hand, or any other task for that matter.

D. B.

Brooklyn, New York
January 2003

NOTES

Cast of Characters

Page xviii "When in the Navy . . ." *Defense Daily* (June 17, 1991), p. 445.

Chapter 1   The Politician, the Businessman, and the Unlucky Eskimos

Page 2 "With a nose for . . ." Interview with Stephen Norris in New York.

Page 2 "Unlike Native Americans . . ." *Washington Monthly* (July 1988), p. 10.

Page 3 "Ask enough people . . ." Interview with Stephen Norris in New York.

Page 4 "He strongly believed . . ." *New Republic* (October 18, 1993).

Page 4 "In the spring of 1980 . . ." Interview with Stephen Norris in New York.

Page 5 "Rubenstein would soon . . ." Interview with Stephen Norris in New York.

Page 7 "The tax loophole . . ." *Washington Monthly* (July 1988), p. 10.

Page 8 "He would later confess . . ." *New Republic* (October 18, 1993).

Page 8 "Arthur Miltenberger . . ." *Forbes* (April 1, 1991), p. 60.

Page 9   "Carlyle took a $35 million . . ." *Washington Post* (February 11, 1998).

Page 10   "In early September . . ." *Washington Post* (September 12, 1988), p. A1.

Page 10   "Norris called Malek . . ." Interview with Stephen Norris in New York.

Page 11   "But after Bush . . ." Interview with Stephen Norris in New York.

Page 11   "Though brief . . ." Phone interview with Fred Malek.

Page 11   "Rubenstein and Conway . . ." Interview with source inside Carlyle.

Chapter 2   Craterair

Page 14   "So in 1989 . . ." *Forbes* (September 26, 1994).

Page 14   "Norris, Malek, and D'Aniello . . ." E-mail interview with Stephen Norris (August 2002).

Page 15   "Caterair consisted . . ." *Washington Post* (July 12, 1989).

Page 16   "By 1990 . . ." Phone interview with Fred Malek.

Page 16   "Northwest needed some help . . ." Interview with Caterair board member.

Page 18   "Norris wasn't making . . ." Interview with Stephen Norris in Washington, DC.

Page 18   "Then Norris went too far . . ." Interview with former Carlyle employee.

Page 19   "Shortly after Norris left . . ." *Dallas Morning News* (September 17, 1994).

Page 20   "Adding injury to insult . . ." *Washington Post* (May 26, 1995).

Page 20   "He offers this . . ." Phone interview with Fred Malek.

Chapter 3   Mr. Clean

Page 23   "Born in Scranton . . ." Frank Carlucci's biography on Defense Department Web site.

Page 25   "'I was never' . . ." *Insight on the News* (August 20, 2001).

Page 25   "Peck says today . . ." *Africa News* (February 19, 2002).

Page 25   "Before being . . ." *The Times* (London; November 8, 1987).

Page 25   "'He has been' . . ." *UPI* (December 3, 1986).

Page 27   "But Hills . . ." Phone interview with Roderick Hills.

Page 28   "Using a subsidiary . . ." *Washington Post* (December 11, 1986).

Page 28   "In the disclosure . . ." *Washington Post* (December 21, 1987).

Page 29   "'Frank has a tremendous' . . ." *National Journal* (February 28, 1987).

Page 29   "Norris says of . . ." Interview with Stephen Norris in New York.

Page 30   "'Frank was washed' . . ." Interview with Stephen Norris in Washington, DC.

Chapter 4   Carlucci's Connections

Page 33   "Carlucci's contacts . . ." Interview with Stephen Norris in New York.

Page 33   "BDM is one of . . ." *Washington Post* (July 4, 1988).

Page 34   "In the spring of . . ." *Los Angeles Times* (July 10, 1988).

Page 35   "Then in the summer . . ." *Defense Daily* (June 17, 1991).

Page 36   "The FBI investigated . . ." *Los Angeles Times* (July 10, 1988).

Page 37   "Ironically, Williams convinced . . ." Interview with Stephen Norris in New York.

Page 38   "A vice chairman . . ." Phone interview with Phil Odeen (August 21, 2002).

Page 38   "On Christmas Eve . . ." *New York Times* (December 24, 1994).

Page 39   "As it turned out . . ." Phone interview with Phil Odeen (August 21, 2002).

Page 40   "Carlyle also used . . ." Interview with Stephen Norris in Washington, DC.

Chapter 5   Getting Defensive

Page 41   "Legendary former chairman . . ." *Washington Post* (March 31, 1985).

Page 42   "The government . . ." *Washington Post* (March 31, 1985).

Page 44   "Then, at 2:30 P.M. . . ." *Harsco* press release (February 2, 1990).

Page 45   "It cost Carlyle . . ." *Fortune* (February 25, 1991).

Page 45   "But in June 1988 . . ." *Washington Post* (September 7, 1991).

Page 46   "The fun once . . ." *Washington Post* (April 19, 1992).

Page 47   "He was a fearsome . . ." Interview with a former Carlyle employee.

Page 49   "Augustine said of the . . ." *Washington Post* (April 19, 1992).

Chapter 6   An Arabian White Knight

Page 53   "Enter the Prince . . ." Interview with Stephen Norris in Washington, DC.

Page 54   "Norris and the Prince . . ." Interview with Stephen Norris in New York.

Page 55   "On February 21 . . ." *Washington Post* (February 22, 1991).

Page 55   "There with the answers . . ." *Washington Post* (February 23, 1991).

Page 57   "After BCCI . . ." *Wall Street Journal* (May 16, 2001).

Page 58   "A source close . . ." Interview with a former financial advisor to Prince Alwaleed.

Chapter 7 Vinnell's Executive Mercenaries

Page 62 "In February 1975 . . ." *Newsweek* (February 24, 1975).

Page 63 "The type of men . . ." *Forbes* (March 1, 1975).

Page 64 "At the time . . ." *Newsweek* (February 24, 1975).

Page 64 "Senator Henry Jackson . . ." *The Associated Press* (March 22, 1997).

Page 66 "Many of its employees . . ." Phone interview with Phil Odeen (August 21, 2002).

Page 66 "In November 1995 . . ." Phone interview with Phil Odeen (August 21, 2002).

Page 67 "According to one . . ." Interview with former Vinnell board member.

Page 68 "William Hartung . . ." *Boston Herald* (December 10, 2001).

Chapter 8 Out of the Shadows

Page 70 "In referring to Carlucci's . . ." Interview with a former Carlyle employee.

Page 71 "Rubenstein, Conway, and Norris . . ." Interview with Stephen Norris in New York.

Page 72 "Then the *New Republic* . . ." *New Republic* (October 18, 1993).

Page 73 "Baker's hiring caused . . ." Interview with a former Carlyle employee.

Page 73 "Carlucci and Baker . . ." Interview with Stephen Norris in New York.

Page 74 "'In the beginning' . . ." Interview with former Carlyle employee.

Page 75 "Without solidarity . . ." Interview with former Carlyle employee.

Page 75 "Norris recalls a painting . . ." Interview with Stephen Norris in New York.

Page 76   "Bill Conway came in . . ." Interview with Stephen Norris in Washington, DC.

Page 77   "His partners were . . ." Interview with Stan Anderson in Washington, DC.

Page 77   "The final straw . . ." Interview with Stephen Norris in Washington, DC, and former Carlyle employees.

Page 77   "After a work out . . ." Phone interview with Antonio Guizzetti.

Page 79   "Rubenstein was quoted . . ." *Washington Post* (January 9, 1995).

Page 79   "Without Norris . . ." Interview with Antonio Guizzetti.

Page 79   "Many people in the . . ." Interview with European banker who did business with both Carlyle and Norris.

Page 79   "To this day . . ." Interview with Stephen Norris in Washington, DC.

Chapter 9   Breaking the Bank

Page 84   "Soros placed . . ." *Times of London* (October 26, 1992).

Page 84   "So an announcement . . ." *Wall Street Journal* (September 27, 1993).

Page 85   "Then in the fall . . ." *Buyouts* (October 9, 1995).

Page 85   "Members of the bin Ladens . . ." Interview with Basil Al Rahim, former Carlyle employee.

Page 85   "And the California . . ." CalPERS Performance Assessment documents (December 31, 2000).

Page 85   "By the time . . ." *Buyouts* (September 30, 1996).

Page 86   "No deal illustrates . . ." *Washington Post* (December 29, 1997).

Page 88   "The company held . . ." *Washington Post* (December 29, 1997).

Page 88   "The money rolled . . ." *Buyouts* (April 6, 1998).

Page 89   "By the end . . ." Carlyle Web site.

Chapter 10 Buying Bush

Page 91 "As Bush campaigned . . ." *Harper's Magazine* (February 2000); *Washington Post* (September 3, 1999); *Wall Street Journal* (September 29, 1999).

Page 92 "According to the Center . . ." Center for Responsive Politics data.

Page 93 "Silvester told . . ." *The Associated Press* (July 21, 1999).

Page 93 "His new boss . . ." *The Associated Press* (July 9, 1999).

Page 94 "The FBI . . ." *The Associated Press* (July 21, 1999).

Page 94 "And finally . . ." *The Hartford Courant* (September 24, 1999).

Page 95 "To this day . . ." Phone interview with Bernard Kavaler (September 2002).

Page 95 "As a result . . ." *The Associated Press* (September 24, 1999).

Page 95 "On September 30, 1999 . . ." Official documents obtained from Connecticut State Treasury department.

Page 98 "The *Wall Street Journal* . . ." *Wall Street Journal* (September 29, 1999).

Page 98 "In addition . . ." *The Associated Press* (January 26, 2000).

Page 99 "In February 2000 . . ." *Harpers Magazine* (February 1, 2000).

Page 101 "However, speculation over . . ." *Too Close to Call: The Thirty-Six Day Battle to Decide the 2000 Election,* Jeffrey Toobin.

Chapter 11 Family Business

Page 107 "In so doing . . ." Phone interview with European investor that did business with Carlyle.

Page 108 "Then in 1998 . . ." Phone interview with former Carlyle employee.

Page 108 "But an Arabic daily . . ." *Agence France Presse* (August 31, 2000).

Page 108 "Baby Bells . . ." *Red Herring* (October 15, 2001).

Page 109 "SBC had not . . ." *Houston Chronicle* (February 15, 2000).

Page 109 "The TPUC . . ." *The Nation* (March 27, 2000).

Page 111 "The *New York Times* . . ." *New York Times* (March 5, 2001).

Page 113 "They say his job . . ." Conversations with Carlyle public relations representative.

Page 113 "Immediately following Bush's . . ." *Korea Economic Weekly* (June 8, 1999).

Page 114 "Carlyle gained approval . . ." *BusinessWeek* (October 30, 2000).

Page 114 "But after some . . ." *BusinessWeek* (October 30, 2000).

Page 115 "Not surprisingly . . ." *The Associated Press* (March 28, 2001).

Page 116 "And the union . . ." *Korea Times* (April 19, 2001).

Page 117 "On June 10, 2001 . . ." *New York Times* (June 10, 2001).

Page 118 "Former employees . . ." Several interviews with former Carlyle employees.

Page 118 "This time the . . ." *New York Times* (July 15, 2001).

Page 119 "The reports of Bush Sr.'s . . ." Phone interview with Tom Fitton (November 2001).

Page 120 "Fitton points out . . ." *New York Times* (July 15, 2001).

Chapter 12   Big Guns

Page 123 "But at the last minute . . ." *Buyouts* (September 15, 1997).

Page 123 "But times had changed . . ." Phone interviews with Andy Krepinevich.

Page 124 "'For the foreseeable' . . ." Phone interviews with Andy Krepinevich.

Page 125 *"Time* magazine . . ." *Time* (January 15, 2001). "While the Crusader won't be ready for action until at least 2008, the kind of war it was meant to fight is already obsolete."

Page 125 "The *Wall Street Journal* . . ." *Wall Street Journal* (May 4, 2001). "The Crusader, which at the time could only be moved by ship, suddenly looked like a dinosaur."

Page 126 " 'We were given' . . ." Phone interview with Doug Coffey.

Page 126 "In the meantime . . ." Information culled from Center for Responsive Politics Web site.

Page 127 "One *Los Angeles Times* . . ." *Los Angeles Times* (January 10, 2002).

Page 127 "Besides, according to . . ." Information culled from Center for Responsive Politics Web site.

Page 128 "'It's impossible' . . ." Phone interview with Peter Eisner.

Page 128 "Regardless of your definition . . ." *Wall Street Journal* (May 4, 2001).

Page 128 "In an interview . . ." Phone interview with Greg McCarthy (November 2001).

Page 128 "One of the lobbyists . . ." Phone interview with former Carlyle lobbyist.

Page 129 "And within 2 months . . ." *Los Angeles Times* (January 10, 2002).

Page 132 " 'BENs has long advocated' . . ." *Aerospace Daily* (July 2, 2001).

Page 135 "This is simply . . ." *Judicial Watch* press release (March 4, 2001).

Chapter 13   9/11/01

Page 140 "George Bush Sr. . . ." Phone conversation with Carlyle spokesperson.

Page 142 "Congress overwhelmingly . . ." *New York Times* (September 22, 2001).

Page 142 "'Capitol Hill' . . ." *New York Times* (September 22, 2001). And before final votes on the 2002 spending plan are even cast, the Pentagon is expected to ask for an additional $15 billion to $25 billion. There is bipartisan support for that, too. "Capitol Hill is prepared to do whatever the Pentagon wants," said Gordon Adams, a budget official in the Clinton administration who is now director of security policy studies at the Elliot School of International Security Studies at George Washington University.

Page 142 "On September 26 . . ." *Los Angeles Times* (January 10, 2002).

Page 143 "'A rising tide' . . ." *New York Times* (September 22, 2001).

Page 143 "On October 22, 2001 . . ." From S-1, an SEC document filed by Carlyle prior to going public.

Page 144 "William Conway . . ." *The Nation* (April 1, 2002).

Page 144 "Nevertheless . . ." *Los Angeles Times* (January 10, 2002).

Page 145 "Carlyle had a relationship . . ." Phone interview with Basil Al Rahim.

Page 146 "Carlyle told the press . . ." *Wall Street Journal* (September 27, 2001).

Page 146 "But one bin Laden . . ." Phone interview with bin Laden family financial advisor.

Page 146 "Regardless of the . . ." *New York Times* (October 26, 2001).

Page 147 "In a March 2002 . . ." *Washington Post* (April 12, 2002).

Page 147 "Carlyle spokesman . . ." *Washington Post* (April 12, 2002).

Page 147 "Representative Johnny Isakson . . ." *Washington Post* (April 12, 2002).

Page 147 "Senator Zell Miller . . ." *San Jose Mercury News* (April 17, 2002).

Page 148 "McKinney would eventually . . ." *Atlanta-Journal-Constitution* (April 15, 2002).

Page 149 "Carlyle owned . . ." *The Associate Press* (December 27, 2001).

Page 150 "In the end . . ." *The Associated Press* (January 16, 2002).

Page 150 "Deep in the belly . . ." *Pittsburgh Business Times Journal* (September 29, 2000).

Page 151 "Employees of the government-run . . ." Interviews with former USIS employees, some over the phone, some over e-mail.

Page 153 "After the unrelenting . . ." *New York Times Magazine* (September 22, 2002).

Page 153 "The actions on the . . ." *The Associated Press* (May 3, 2002). Rumsfeld told reporters Thursday he was disturbed by reports that Army officials had gone behind his back to Congress in hopes that politics would overpower policy and save the Crusader artillery program. "I have a minimum of high regard for that kind of behavior," Rumsfeld said.

Page 153 " 'United Defense' . . ." United Defense press release (August 9, 2002).

Page 154 "The deal happened . . ." *New Internationalist Magazine* (July 1, 2002).

Epilogue

Page 157 "Fiona Draper . . ." *Guardian Unlimited* (September 5, 2002).

Page 157 "When Carlyle was . . ." Interview with former Carlyle employee.

BIBLIOGRAPHY

Chapter 1   The Politician, the Businessman, and the Unlucky Eskimos

Berss, Marci. "If at First You Don't Succeed." *Forbes,* April 1, 1991, p. 60.

Gladwell, Malcolm. "Fairchild Bid Raised by Carlyle." *Washington Post,* February 1, 1989, p. F1.

Greene, Robert. "Bush Appointee Resigns Over 'Cabal' Report." *Associated Press,* September 12, 1988.

Groves, Martha. "Sears Said Close to Selling Unit of Coldwell Banker." *Los Angeles Times,* March 14, 1989.

Hoffman, David. "Bush Associate Resigns after Disclosure on BLS; Malek Tallied Jews for Nixon Administration." *Washington Post,* September 12, 1988, p. A1.

Knight, Jerry. "A Big-Money Matchmaker; Thayer Capital Makes Its Mark as a New Player Among Old-Time Investment Firms." *Washington Post,* June 29, 1998, p. F12.

Lewis, Michael. "The Access Capitalists; Influence Peddling: The Next Generation." *New Republic,* October 18, 1993, p. 20.

Mintz, John. "So What Would Your Company Do With These Guys on Your Team?" *Washington Post,* April 7, 1996, p. H1.

Ortega, Bob. "Ice Fishing; How Pillsbury, Quaker Oats, and Drexel Burnham Got Millions in Cool Cash from Alaska's Eskimos." *Washington Monthly,* July 1988, p. 10.

Sugawara, Sandra. "Carlyle's $75 million Offer Accepted By N.J. Company." *Washington Post,* September 30, 1988, p. 3.

Swardson, Anne. "Aleut Alert: Firms Eye Tax Loopholes in Alaskan Concerns." *Washington Post,* October 21, 1986, p. C1.

Turner, Robert. "A Wrong That Must Be Acknowledged." *Boston Globe,* December 8, 1991, p. A25.

Warren Walsh, Sharon. "Rafshoon's TV Production Firm Is Acquired." *Washington Post,* February 11, 1988, p. 10.

Weintraub, Bernard. "New Job For Aide Who Quit Bush Campaign." *New York Times,* September 10, 1989, p. 21.

Chapter 2   Craterair

"Caterair International Files to Sell $230 Mln of Notes." *Bloomberg News,* July 14, 1993.

Ewen, Beth. "Malek Brings Cargo of Controversy to NWA." *Minneapolis-St. Paul CityBusiness,* October 9, 1989, p. 1.

Faiola, Anthony. "Onex to Take Over Caterair Operations." *Washington Post,* May 11, 1995, p. B14.

Farhi, Paul. "Marriott's Air Catering Unit Is Sold." *Washington Post,* July 12, 1989, p. F1.

Field, David. "Malek Reduces His Role at Northwest Airlines." *Washington Times,* June 20, 1990, p. C1.

Kamen, Al. "It Takes More than Two." *Washington Post,* May 26, 1995, p. A25.

Prakash, Snigdha. "Caterair International Spreads Its Wings on a Solo Flight." *Washington Post,* August 3, 1992, p. 5.

Rotenier, Nancy. "Coffee, Tea, or Bankruptcy?" *Forbes,* September 26, 1994, p. 72.

Slater, Wayne. "Bush Defends Leaving Troubled Firm's Board." *Dallas Morning News,* September 17, 1994, p. 40A.

Chapter 3   Mr. Clean

Auerback, Stuart. "Sears Tries New Role as Wheeler-Dealer in World Trade." *Washington Post,* April 9, 1984, p. 1.

Cockburn, Alexander. "Creepy Carlucci; Frank Carlucci: Beat the Devil." *Nation,* December 20, 1986, p. 694.

"Congo-Kinshasa: The Cardinal Sin That Lumumba Committed." *Africa News,* February 19, 2002.

Day, Kathleen. "Frank Carlucci and the Corporate Whirl." *Washington Post,* February 7, 1993, p. H1.

Dizard, John. "Sears' Humbled Trading Empire." *Fortune,* June 25, 1984, p. 71.

"Frank C. Carlucci: 16th Secretary of Defense, Reagan Administration." Department of Defense, www.defenselink.mil.

"Frank Charles Carlucci: New National Security Adviser." *U.P.I.,* December 2, 1986.

"Frank Charles Carlucci." *Washington Post,* November 6, 1987, p. A14.

Kirschten, Dick. "Competent Manager." *National Journal,* February 28, 1987, p. 468.

Komisar, Lucy. "Carlucci Can't Hide His Role in 'Lumumba.'" *Pacific News Service,* February 14, 2002.

Mayer, Caroline E. "Carlucci Supersvised Arms Advisers at Sears." *Washington Post,* December 11, 1986, p. A1.

Mayer, Caroline E. "Sears Trade Takes on a Smaller Chunk of the World." *Washington Post,* October 14, 1985, p. F3.

Moore, Molly. "Corporate Post Made Carlucci Rich." *Washington Post,* December 21, 1987, p. A5.

Morley, Jefferson. "Story of a Consummate Bureaucrat, Frank C. Carlucci." *Nation,* December 19, 1987, p. 737.

"President Calls on a Mr. Clean." *Chicago Tribune,* December 3, 1986, p. 1.

"Profile on Frank Carlucci: From the Knives of the Congo to Darkest Pentagon." *Times* (London), November 8, 1987.

Shorrock, Tim. "Company Man." *Nation,* March 14, 2002.

Chapter 4　Carlucci's Connections

Gerth, Jeff. "In a Shadowy Marketplace, America Buys Russian Arms." *New York Times*, December 24, 1994, p. 1.

Gibbons, Kent. "Auditing Consultant Named to Head BDM." *Washington Times*, March 10, 1992, p. C1.

Goodwin, William. "Loral Corp. in Pact with Carlyle Group on Sale of Ford Aerospace Assets." *American Banker*, September 19, 1990, p. 22.

Jehl, Douglas and William C. Rempel. "Firm Saw Big Jump in Navy Contracts after Hiring Paisley's Wife." *Los Angeles Times*, July, 10, 1988, p. 30.

Obituaries "Melvyn Paisley, 77, Navy Aide Caught in Procurement Scandal." *Los Angeles Times*, December 27, 2001, p. 11.

"Paisley Pleads Guilty to Ill Wind Conspiracy." *Defense Daily*, June 17, 1991, p. 445.

Sugawara, Sandra. "Carlyle Group to Buy BDM." *Washington Post*, September 19, 1990, p. 1.

Sugawara, Sandra. "Secret of Success for BDM May Be President's Style." *Washington Post*, July 4, 1988, p. 1.

Chapter 5　Getting Defensive

Atkinson, Rick and Fred Hiatt. "Contracting Conducted Over Golden Safety Net." *Washington Post*, March 31, 1985, p. A1.

Colodny, Mark M. "Frank Carlucci Goes Hunting." *Fortune*, February 25, 1991, p. 155.

Field, David. "Harsco Spurns Carlyle Proposal." *Washington Times*, April 25, 1990, p. C3.

Friedman, Alan. "Big Names at Little-Known Investment House." *Financial Times*, September 30, 1993, p. 27.

"Harsco Corp. Announcement." *PR Newswire*, February 2, 1990.

Hinden, Stan. "Carlyle Puts Heat on Harsco." *Washington Post*, April 12, 1990, p. 1.

Howe, Robert F. "Unisys to Pay Record Fine in Defense Fraud." *Washington Post,* September 7, 1991, p. 1.

Morrison, David C. "Eat or Be Eaten." *National Journal,* March 6, 1993, p. 559.

Pearlstein, Steven. "Loral, Northrop, Carlyle Win Bidding War for LTV Unit." *Washington Post,* August 14, 1992, p. B1.

Pearlstein, Steven. "Opposition to LTV Bid Intensifies; Congress, Bush Panel Fault Thomson Deal." *Washington Post,* July 3, 1992, p. F1.

Pearlstein, Steven. "Undoing a Done Deal: How a Few Key Days Broke Marietta's Grip on LTV Aerospace." *Washington Post,* April 19, 1992, p. H1.

Smith, Todd. "Carlyle Offers Harsco Peace Pact." *Washington Times,* January 18, 1991, p. C7.

Chapter 6   An Arabian White Knight

"BCCI Behind Closed Doors." *Financial Times* (London), November 16, 1991, p. 4.

Day, Kathleen. "Citicorp Deal Puts Saudi in Kind of Situation He Hoped to Avoid." *Washington Post,* February 23, 1991, p. B1.

Day, Kathleen. "Saudi Invests $590 million in Citicorp." *Washington Post,* February 22, 1991, p. 1.

Frank, Steve. "Prince Alwaleed's Road to Riches." *Wall Street Journal,* May 16, 2001.

Knight, Jerry. "Saudi Billionaire Discloses Investments of $850 million; Motorola, News Corp., Netscape Buys Cited." *Washington Post,* November 26, 1997, p. C9.

LaFraniere, Sharon. "Grand Jury Indicts BCCI in alifornia Bank Takeover." *Washington Post,* November 16, 1991, p. 1.

Chapter 7   Vinnell's Executive Mercenaries

Gibbons, Kent. "BDM Swallows Vinnell of Fairfax." *Washington Times,* March 14, 1992, p. B5.

Hanley, Charles J. "Saudi Guard Gets Quiet Help from U.S. Firm with Connections." *Associated Press,* March 22, 1997.

"Mideast Dilemma: Is U.S. Training a Future Foe?" *U.S. News & World Report,* February 24, 1975, p. 21.

Priest, Dana. "Attack Puts Spotlight on American Presence." *Washington Post,* November 14, 1995, p. A15.

Schrader, Esther. "Companies Capitalize on War on Terror; Since the 1970s, the U.S. Has Used Private Contractors to Educate Foreign Troops." *Los Angeles Times,* April 14, 2002, p. 1A.

Silverstein, Ken. "Saudis and Americans: Friends in Need." *Nation,* December 3, 2001, p. 15.

Stacks, John F. "The Marine's Private Army; Former Spooks and Oddball Operatives Made up North's Band." *Time,* July 13, 1987, p. 32.

"Terrorism against Energy Pipelines." *Defense & Foreign Affairs Daily,* June 13, 2002.

"The U.S. Foreign Legion." *Forbes,* March 1, 1975, p. 40.

Well, Jonathan, Jack Meyers, and Maggie Mulvihill. "War on Terrorism: U.S. Ties to Saudi Elite May Be Hurting War on Terrorism." *Boston Herald,* December 10, 2001, p. 1.

Willenson, Kim. "Persian Gulf: This Gun for Hire." *Newsweek,* February 24, 1975, p. 30.

Chapter 8   Out of the Shadows

Alexander, Garth. "How Reagan's Aides Rescued Euro Disney." *Sunday Times,* June 12, 1994.

Friedman, Alan. "Big Names at Little-Known Investment House." *Financial Times,* September 30, 1993, p. 27.

Greenwald, John. "Peddling Power for Profit; Big Names and Political Connections Prove a Bankable Asset for a Growing Washington Investment Firm." *Time,* March 22, 1993, p. 39.

"James Baker to Join Carlyle Group as Partner." *Bloomberg News,* March 11, 1993.

"Kuwaiti Oil Company Buys 300 Agip Service Stations." *Agence France Presse,* September 6, 1995.

Lacayo, Richard. "The Rebellious Soldier; Unable to March in Step with His New Commander in Chief, Colin Powell Mulls Over His Postmilitary Options." *Time,* February 15, 1993, p. 32.

Lewis, Michael. "The Access Capitalists; Influence Peddling: The Next Generation." *New Republic,* October 18, 1993, p. 20.

Mintz, John. "Founder Going Beyond the Carlyle Group; Norris to Start Investment Partnership." *Washington Post,* January 9, 1995, p. F9.

"Richard Darman to Join Carlyle Group as a Managing Director." *Bloomberg News,* February 24, 1993.

Chapter 9   Breaking the Bank

"Carlyle Adds to Fund in Second Closing." *Buyouts,* January 9, 1995.

"Carlyle Boosts Target, Sets November Final." *Buyouts,* October 9, 1995.

"Carlyle Fund Nears $300 Million First Close." *Buyouts,* September 12, 1994.

"Carlyle Fund Rolls to $1.33 Billion Final." *Buyouts,* September 30, 1996.

"Carlyle Group Nearing Fund Closing." *Mergers & Acquisitions Report,* December 6, 1993.

"Carlyle Group Raises $1.1 Billion for European Buyout Fund." *Bloomberg News,* July 30, 1998.

Cook, Bob. "Carlyle Fund Reaches $400 Million." *Mergers & Acquisitions Report,* December 12, 1994, p. 3.

Harlan, Christi. "Carlyle Group's Fund Gets Stake from George Soros." *Wall Street Journal,* September 27, 1993.

Jury, Jennifer. "Carlyle Caps Europe Fund at Double Its Initial Target." *U.K. Venture Capital Journal,* October 1, 1998.

Kaletsky, Anatole. "How Mr. Soros Made a Billion By Betting against the Pound." *Times* (London), October 26, 1992.

Kosman, Josh. "Carlyle Expands Reach with Latin, Russian Funds." *Buyouts,* June 1, 1998.

Kosman, Josh. "Carlyle, Now Global, Turns Attention to Asia with New Mega-Fund." *Buyouts,* April 20, 1998.

Kosman, Josh. "Carlyle Raises $1 Billion for First European Fund." *Buyouts,* April 6, 1998.

Kosman, Josh. "Politicos on the Buyout Bandwagon." *Global Finance,* May 1, 1998.

Moriarty, George. "Carlyle Opens New Investment Avenues." *Private Equity Week,* May 4, 1998.

Pearlstein, Steven. "Carlyle's Good Fortune; with Incentives, the Art of the Deal Becomes a Billion-Dollar Bonanza." *Washington Post,* December 29, 1997, p. F10.

"Soros to Invest $100 million in Carlyle Group U.S. Investment Fund." *Bloomberg News,* September 27, 1993.

"Thiokol, Carlyle Group Joining Forces to Buy Howmet Corp." *Weekly Business of Aviation,* October 16, 1995.

"Winning Big from Collapse of Pound." *Financial Post,* October 27, 1992.

Chapter 10   Buying Bush

Concson, Joe and Kevin P. Phillips. "The George W. Bush Success Story; A Heartwarming Tale about Baseball, $1.7 Billion, and a Lot of Swell Friends." *Harper's Magazine,* February 1, 2000, p. 39.

"Former Treasurer Leaves New Job in Midst of Federal Probe." *Associated Press,* July 9, 1999.

Fulman, Ricki. "Paul Silvester out at New Job with Washington Consultant." *Pensions and Investments,* July 26, 1999, p. 4.

Gorlick, Adam. "Bush Money Man Steps Aside, for Now." *Associated Press,* September 24, 1999.

Lender, Jon. "Associate of Former Treasurer Cooperates in Probe; Finder's Fees Key Focus in Silvester Investigation." *Hartford Courant,* September 4, 1999, p. A1.

Lender, Jon. "Companies Warned on Finder's Fees." *Hartford Courant,* November 9, 1999.

Lender, Jon. "Nappier Releases List of 'Finders': Top Politicians Linked to Pension Fund Deals." *Hartford Courant,* October 21, 1999, p. A1.

Lender, Jon. "SEC Probe Likely Partnership Invested State Pension Funds." *Hartford Courant,* December 9, 1999.

Lender, Jon. "3 Plead Guilty in Corruption Case." *Hartford Courant,* September 24, 1999, p. A1.

Mintz, John. "State Pension Investments Probed; Ex-Conn. Treasurer Placed Funds with Firms Tied to Bush Fund Raiser." *Washington Post,* September 3, 1999, p. A25.

"Nappier Reveals Compensation Paid By Firms in Response to Her Request for Disclosure." Office of Connecticut State Treasurer Denise Nappier, October 20, 1999.

"Office of Ex-Treasurer's Sister Searched by FBI." *Associated Press,* July 21, 1999.

Rhodes, Tom. "Bush's Backers in Fraud Inquiry." *Sunday Times* (London), March 5, 2000.

"Some Figures in Texas Flap Linked to Silvester." *Associated Press,* March 7, 2000.

Starkman, Dean. "Connecticut Treasurer Moves to Unwind or Cancel Investments Made By Silvester." *Wall Street Journal,* September 29, 1999.

"Statement by State Treasurer Denise L. Nappier." Office of Connecticut State Treasurer Denise Nappier, November 16, 1999.

"$3 Million in Fees Paid to Carlyle Group Subsidiary." *Journal Inquirer of Manchester,* January 26, 2000.

"Treasurer Updates Compensation Disclosure Report." Office of Connecticut State Treasurer Denise Nappier, December 8, 1999.

Zielbauer, Paul. "Connecticut Ex-Treasurer Jailed." *New York Times,* January 3, 2002, p. B4.

Chapter 11 Family Business

"A Media Specialist Is Leaving Salomon." *New York Times,* June 19, 1998, p. D4.

"Carlyle-KorAm Deal Faces Tough Challenges." *Korea Times,* March 17, 2000.

Corn, David and Paul Lashmar. "Bush of Arabia; Questions about Former President George Bush and Former Prime Minister John Major Traveling to Saudi Arabia on Behalf of the Carlyle Group." *Nation,* March 27, 2000, p. 19.

Davidson, Paul. "Phone Start-Ups Tangle with Giants." *USA Today,* August 21, 2001, p. 1B.

"Ex-U.S. Pres. Bush Arrives in Seoul." *Korea Times,* May 28, 1999.

"Former FCC Chairman Kennard to Join Carlyle." *Wall Street Journal,* May 3, 2001, p. C16.

Fowler, Tom. "SBC to Offer Long Distance as of July 10; FCC Approval to Heat up Telecom Market in Texas." *Houston Chronicle,* July 1, 2000, p. 1.

Gedda, George. "Out of Sync Seoul." *Associated Press,* March 28, 2001.

Ihlwan, Moon. "The Bank That Almost Got Away." *BusinessWeek,* October 30, 2000, p. 58.

Khanthong, Thanong. "Anand Outlines Ties to Group of Giants." *Nation,* March 6, 2001.

"KorAm Major Sharholder Carlyle Is Speculative Investor." *Korea Times,* April 19, 2001.

Marquis, Christopher. "Experts Urge Bush to Resume North Korea Talks." *New York Times,* March 27, 2001.

Miller, Alan C. "Problems with a Globe-Trotting Father; Ex-President Bush's Many Foreign Dealings Could Pose Conflicts If His Son Wins White House." *Los Angeles Times,* May 7, 2000, p. 1A.

Mowbray, Rebecca. "Justice Weighs in against SBC Bid; FTC to Make Decision By April." *Houston Chronicle,* February 15, 2000, p. 1.

"North Korea: U.S. Plans to Resume Talks." *Facts on File World News Digest,* June 6, 2001.

Perlez, Jane. "Bush Senior, on His Son's Behalf, Reassures Saudi Leader." *New York Times,* July 15, 2001, p. 6.

Perlez, Jane. "Fatherly Advice to the President on North Korea." *New York Times,* June 10, 2001.

"SBC Can Offer Long-Distance to 2 States." *Houston Chronicle,* January 23, 2001.

"SBC Communications, Saudi's STC Break off Partnership Talks." *Agence France Presse,* December 13, 2000.

"U.S. Carlyle to Invest over $1 Billion." Korea Times, May 28, 1999.

"U.S. Firm to Link with Saudi Phone Company." *Agence France Presse,* August 31, 2000.

Wayne, Leslie. "Elder Bush in Big G.O.P. Cast Toiling for Top Equity Firm." *New York Times,* March 5, 2001.

Chapter 12   Big Guns

Barry, John. "Choose Your Weapons." *Newsweek,* May 20, 2002, p. 43.

"Bush Sr. Should Stop Working for International Equity Firm While Son Is President." *Judicial Watch,* March 4, 2001.

"Business Briefs." *Chicago Tribune,* August 13, 1997, p. 3.

"Business in Brief." *Washington Post,* December 5, 2000, p. E2.

Fisher, Ian. "Montenegro: Voters Back Leader's Party." *New York Times,* May 17, 2002, p. A6.

Graham, Bradley. "Army Plans Modest Makeover of Combat Divisions." *Washington Post,* June 9, 1998, p. A1.

"Harsco, FMC Sign Definitive Agreement to Sell United Defense, L.P. to the Carlyle Group." *PR Newswire,* August 26, 1997.

Jaffe, Greg and Anne Marie Squeo. "Heavy Metal: Crusader Artillery Gun Becomes the Quarry in Pentagon Showdown." *Wall Street Journal,* May 4, 2001, p. A1.

"Judicial Watch to File FOIA Lawsuit Today over Carlyle Group Documents." *Judicial Watch,* November 27, 2001.

Kosman, Josh. "Carlyle Takes a Shot with $850 Million Defense Buy-out." *Buyouts,* September 15, 1997.

"Missiles and Summitry: A Farewell to Armaments." *Economist,* May 18, 2002, p. 29.

Mulvihill, Maggie, Jack Meyers, and Jonathan Wells. "Slick Deals: Bush Advisers Cashed in on Saudi Gravy Train." *Boston Herald,* December 11, 2001, p. 1.

Newman, Rick. "Study Warns Army Lowering Standards for Vehicles." *Defense Week,* March 6, 2000.

"Rumsfeld Taking Defense Budget in Right Direction, BENS Says." *Aerospace Daily,* July 2, 2001, p. 1.

Schneider, Greg and Thomas E. Ricks. "Firms to Build Lighter Army Vehicles." *Washington Post,* November 17, 2000, p. E3.

"Technology Network Hosts Event for Texas Governor George W. Bush." *Business Wire,* September 30, 1999.

Thompson, Mark. "Blasting the Crusader: Why the Army's Newest and Biggest Gun May Become a Target for Bush's Defense Department." *Time,* January 15, 2001, p. 34.

Chapter 13   9/11/01

"Anthrax Cleanup Jobs Awarded." *Engineering News Record,* November 12, 2001, p. 15.

"Army Issues Notice of Crusader Contract Cancellation; United Defense Awarded Contract to Develop New Cannon Artillery System for the U.S. Army." *PR Newswire,* August 9, 2002.

"Bin Laden Family Is Tied to U.S. Group." *Wall Street Journal,* September 27, 2001, p. A3.

Brazaitis, Tom. "A Strange Intersection of Bushes and Bin Ladens." *Plain Dealer of Cleveland,* November 13, 2001.

Burns, Robert. "Army Probes Alleged Weapon Lobbying." *Associated Press,* May 3, 2002.

"Chronology of Anthrax Events." *Sun-Sentinel,* January 10, 2002.

Clow, Robert. "The Well-Connected Deal-Makers." *Financial Times* (London), August 26, 2002, p. 10.

"Company Agrees to Acquire Environmental Firm." *Associated Press,* January 16, 2002.

Corn, David. "Crusader: Intrigue and Backstabbing in the House of Bush." *Nation,* May 6, 2002.

Dao, James. "The Military Contractors; Beneficiaries of the Military Buildup Await Their Orders." *New York Times,* September 22, 2001, p. C1.

"DOD to Cancel Controversial Crusader Program." News Briefs From U.S. Congresswoman Cynthia McKinney, May 8, 2002.

Edsall, Thomas B. "Muslims Aid Embattled House Member." *Washington Post,* August 2, 2002, p. A6.

Eichenwald, Kurt. "Bin Laden Family Liquidates Holdings with Carlyle Group." *New York Times,* October 26, 2001.

Eilperin, Juliet. "Democrat Implies Sept. 11 Administration Plot." *Washington Post,* April 12, 2002, p. A16.

Finelli, Frank. "The Crusader and Defense Transformation." *Defense Week,* May 28, 2002.

Fineman, Mark. "Arms Buildup Is a Boon to Firm Run by Big Guns; Ex-President and Other Washington Elites Are Behind the Carlyle Group." *Los Angeles Times,* January 10, 2002, p. A1.

"IT Group Says Debt Refinancing Unlikely, Considering Chapter 11." *Associated Press,* December 27, 2001.

McKay, Jim. "On the Prowl; Cleanup Company to Move Here, Seek Acquisitions." *Pittsburgh Post-Gazette,* January 5, 1997, p. C5.

McKinney, Cynthia. "Bush Must Answer Sept. 11 Questions." *Atlanta Journal-Constitution,* April 15, 2002, p. 10A.

"Mountain Men." *Pittsburgh Business Times Journal,* September 29, 2000, p. 3.

Nisse, Jason. "Bush Faces Flak over Family Links with Winner of U.S. Defence Contract." *Independent on Sunday* (London), January 13, 2002, p. 1.

Parker, Kathleen. "Idiotic Accusation Borders on Treason." *San Jose Mercury News,* April 17, 2002, p. FEA.

Pincus, Walter. "Crusader a Boon to Carlyle Group Even If Pentagon Scraps Project." *Washington Post,* May 14, 2002, p. A3.

"September 11: Chronology of Terror." CNN.com, September 12, 2001.

Shorrock, Tim. "Crony Capitalism Goes Global." *Nation,* April 1, 2002.

Shorrock, Tim. "The Big Guns." *New Internationalist Magazine,* July 1, 2002.

Shuler, Dearda. "Has Terrorism Come to the U.S. or Has It Always Been Here?" *Michigan Citizen,* October 13, 2001, p. 10.

"The IT Group Is Providing Widespread Support for the Anthrax Response." *PR Newswire,* November 20, 2001.

Thompson, Mark. "The Lessons of Afghanistan." *Time,* February 18, 2002, p. 28.

Ward, Mike. "Bin Laden Relatives Have Ties to Texas." *Austin American-Statesman,* November 9, 2001, p. A1.

Woolner, Ann. "The Truth Behind Congresswoman's 9/11 Conspiracy." *Bloomberg News,* May 24, 2002.

Epilogue

Almon, Siobhan. "QinetiQ Agency to Go Private." *Daily Deal,* January 22, 2002.

"Congress Told of $520 Million in Taiwan Military Sales." *Reuters,* September 5, 2002.

Pank, Philip. "MOD Rejects Fears over Defence Sell-Off." *Guardian,* September 5, 2002.

Shorrock, Tim. "U.S.-Taiwan; The Guiding Hand of Frank Carlucci." *Asia Times,* March 19, 2002.

Wonacott, Peter. "Private-Equity Funds Launch Oversight Association in China." *Wall Street Journal,* June 18, 2002.

INDEX